Favorite
Prayers from the Bible

Jesus, just as You taught the Apostles
to pray, teach us to pray from the Bible.

FAVORITE
PRAYERS FROM THE BIBLE

Edited by
Rev. Francis Evans

Illustrated

CATHOLIC BOOK PUBLISHING CO.
New Jersey

NIHIL OBSTAT: Francis J. McAree, S.T.D.
Censor Librorum

IMPRIMATUR: ✛ Patrick J. Sheridan, D.D.
Vicar General, Archdiocese of New York

The Nihil Obstat and Imprimatur are official declarations that a book or a pamphlet is free of doctrinal or moral error. No implication is contained therein that those who have granted the Nihil Obstat and Imprimatur agree with the contents, opinions, or statements expressed.

(T-925)

CONTENTS

FOREWORD

One of the most important aims of the Second Vatican Council was to open the Scriptures to the faithful, especially through the Liturgy: "The treasures of the Bible are to be opened more lavishly, so that richer fare may be provided for the faithful at the table of God's Word" (*Constitution on the Sacred Liturgy*, no. 51).

The Council went further and indicated that the prayer life of the faithful should be based on the Bible: "[The faithful] should gladly put themselves in contact with the sacred text [of the Bible], whether it be through the sacred Liturgy . . . or through devotional reading. . . .

"And let them remember that prayer should accompany the reading of sacred Scripture, so that God and humans may talk together; for we speak to Him when we pray; we listen to Him when we read the Divine sayings" (*Constitution on Divine Revelation,* no. 25).

It is clear then that the Bible is the Catholic prayerbook par excellence. Not only does it encourage and lead to prayer but it also contains some of the most beautiful prayers that we have at our disposal. Rightly has the Bible been termed the Prayerbook of the Holy Spirit!

The present book is intended to help Catholics make use of some of the best prayers of the Bible. By utilizing it, they can pray in the words of the great personages of the Faith, the universal and timeless sentiments of the Psalms, the very prayers of the Lord Jesus, and the devout prayers of the early Church.

At the same time, the prayers represented herein deal with many of the most important concerns of life. They can be used with full confidence that they will enhance the spiritual life of Catholics today.

At times, however, the "prayers" do not speak *to* God but *of* God. Yet they are so filled with His presence that they become true prayers for us. Such prayers call upon our brothers and sisters in the Faith, other people in general, and all creation to adore, thank, and praise God.

Some prayers make use of the plural "us" instead of the singular "me." The reason is obvious: each believer (whether he or she knows it or not) always prays *with* the whole Church and *in the name of* the Church. At the same time, Christians regard words such as "Israel" and "people" (which occur frequently in these Bible prayers) as synonyms for the *Church*.

Every effort has been made to ensure that this book will be easy to use and attractive to the person praying. The text is printed in large pleasing typeface and in red and black. The inspiring colorful illustrations will help keep our minds on Jesus and through Him on the other Persons of the Blessed Trinity.

May all who use this prayerbook achieve a deeper and more vital spiritual life. May it lead them ever closer to the eternal union with the living God.

MOSES—POWERFUL EXEMPLAR OF PRAYER

The prayer life of the Israelites was typified by leaders such as Moses. By communing with God in the burning bush and on the holy mountain (for forty days and nights), he set an example of how the individual Israelites should pray to God.

PRAYERS IN THE HISTORY OF ISRAEL
(OLD TESTAMENT)

*T*HE *dialogue of human beings with God is so natural and spontaneous that it existed from the very beginning of the human race. The Old Testament writers acknowledged that God was infinitely superior to humans and could not be compelled to answer prayers by incantations, exorcisms, or magical formulas, and so they prohibited use of such superstitious obligations.*

Thus, Israel surpassed all the ancient religions in its unique concept of God and its life of prayer. Prayer is directed to God alone in the Old Testament, and all Israelites are encouraged to make prayer an essential part of their religious obligations.

The most characteristic element of Old Testament prayer is its relation to the saving plan of God: people pray, beginning with what has happened or with what is happening, so that something may happen and God's salvation may be granted to the earth. All of sacred history is marked by prayer; the high points are punctuated by the prayer of the mediators and the whole people, who depend on the knowledge of the plan of God to obtain His intervention in the present moment.

Public prayer is exercised by leaders and kings, such as Moses, David, and Solomon; prophets, like Elijah, Samuel, and Jeremiah; religious leaders, such as Ezra and Nehemiah; and freedom fighters, like Judas Maccabeus. Personal prayer is practiced by many different individuals, such as Jonah, Tobit, Judith, Esther, and Job.

The Church encourages us to make all these prayers our own, since they are found in her own book, the Bible, which is inspired by the Holy Spirit, and they can add much knowledge and devotion to our lives

PRAYERS OF LEADERS AND KINGS

Prayer of Moses

Hymn of victory after the crossing of the Red Sea

I will offer praise to the Lord,
for He has been triumphant and shown
forth His glory;
horse and chariot He has hurled into the
sea.
The Lord is the source of my strength and
my courage;
He has been my Savior.
The Lord is my God, and I offer Him
praise;
He is the God of my father, and I sing of His
marvelous deeds.
The Lord has proved Himself a warrior;
Lord is His Name.
The chariots and the army of Pharaoh He
cast into the sea.

At a breath of Your anger the waters cas-
caded;
the waters ceased to flow and converged together,
forming a barrier in the midst of the sea.
The enemy had boasted:
"We will relentlessly pursue them,
and when we overtake them,

we will divide the spoils and be satiated with
   them;
we will draw our swords and gather up
   their plunder."
But when You caused the wind to blow, the
   sea swept over them;
they sank like lead in the swirling waters.

Who can compare to You among the gods,
   O Lord?
Who can begin to comprehend how magnificent is Your holiness?
O worker of wonders, Whose renown is in-
   comparable,
when You stretched out Your right hand,
   the earth consumed our enemies.
You showed Your mercy by leading the people You had redeemed;
You proved Your strength by guiding them
   to Your holy dwelling.
Then You brought them in
and gave them the mountain of Your inheritance as their dwelling—
the place that You chose for Your throne, O
   Lord,
the sanctuary established by Your hands.
The Lord shall rule forever and ever.

Exodus 15:1-4a, 8-13, 17-18

Prayer of Hannah

The humble find joy in God

MY heart sings praise to the Lord,
my strength is exalted because of my God.
I have disposed of my enemies;
my victory is the cause of my joy.

There is no one to equal the Lord in holiness;
there is no Rock to match our God.
Never again dare to speak boastfully
or allow an arrogant thought to escape your
lips.
For the Lord our God knows all things,
and He judges deeds accordingly.

The weapons of the mighty have been destroyed,
while those who are weak grow stronger
with each passing day.
Those who did not lack for food now seek
work that will afford them bread,
while those who were hungry now eat their
fill.
The wife who was barren now brings forth
seven sons,
while the mother of many has become un-
fruitful.

The Lord is the source of both death and
life;

He casts down to the netherworld and He raises up again.

The Lord permits some to be poor, others to be rich;

He humbles, but He also exalts.

The Lord raises those who are needy from the dust of the earth;

from the refuse heap He lifts up the poor,

to associate them with those of noble birth

and give them a glorious throne as their heritage.

For the earth's foundations are the Lord's,

and He has established the world upon them.

He will guard the life journey of those who are His faithful servants,

but He will allow the wicked to perish in the darkness.

For not by power does one prevail;

those who oppose the Will of the Lord shall be abandoned.

The Most High in heaven shows forth His power;

the Lord judges the earth in its entirety.

May He now deign to give strength to His king

and exalt the power of His anointed.

1 Samuel 2:1-10

Prayer of David

Thanksgiving for God's goodness

Who am I, Lord God,
that You have honored me and the members of my house so greatly?
Yet even this You regard as too little, Lord God;
You have also said that the house of Your servant
will endure for many generations. . . .
What further can I say to You?
You know Your servant, Lord God.
For the sake of Your servant and in accordance with Your Divine Will,
You have completely revealed Your magnificent design to Your servant.

And so I pray:
You are great, Lord God.
No one is equal to You,
and there is no God but You,
just as has been revealed to us.
What other nation on earth can be compared to Your people Israel,
which You have led, redeeming it as Your own possession?
You have thereby made Yourself renowned through this magnificent deed,
as well as by other awe-inspiring acts,

as You have removed the obstacles of hostile nations
and their gods from the path of Your people,
which You have redeemed from Egypt as
Your special possession.

You have established Your people as Yours
forever, O Lord,
and You have become their God.
And now, Lord God, I ask You to confirm
for all time
the Covenant You have made concerning
Your servant and his house,
and to fulfill Your promise.
Your name will be forever exalted
when people say, "The Lord of Hosts is the
God of Israel,"
and the house of Your servant David stands
firm in Your presence.
You, Lord of Hosts, God of Israel,
revealed to Your servant:
"I will build a house for you."
Only because of this does Your servant now
find the courage
to make this prayer to You.

Lord God, You are our God and Your words
radiate truth;
You have made this gracious promise to
Your servant.

Therefore I beg You to bless the house of
    Your servant
so that it may stand firm in Your presence
    forever.
For You, Lord God, have revealed Your
    Will,
and as the result of Your blessing the house
    of Your servant shall be blessed forever.

2 Samuel 7:18-29

Prayer of Solomon

May God heed the petitions of His people

O Lord, God of Israel,
there exists no god who is Your equal
in heaven above or on earth below.
You remain faithful to Your Covenant of
    kindness with Your servants
who follow You with their complete heart.
Is it truly possible
that God has chosen to dwell among human
    beings on earth?
If the highest heavens are unable to contain
    You,
how can this temple possibly do so?

Regard with mercy the prayer and petition
    of Your servant,
O Lord, my God,
and pay heed to my plea of supplication

with which I, Your servant, approach You
    today.
May Your eyes continue to watch day and
    night over this temple,
the place where You have decreed that
    honor shall be paid to You.
I implore You to heed the prayer
that I, Your servant, offer here today.
I beg You to look with favor on the prayer
    of Your servant
and on the petition of Your people.
Please listen to them whenever they call
    upon You,
for You have designated them among all the
    peoples of the earth
for Your special inheritance.

1 Kings 8:23, 27-29, 52-53

Prayer of Jehoshaphat

Call for help in time of trouble

O Lord, God of our fathers,
are You not the God in heaven
Who rules over all the kingdoms of the na-
    tions?
Are power and might not in Your hand
so that no one can withstand You?
Was it not You, O God, Who drove out
    those who dwelt in this land

when they were confronted by Your people
Israel,
and did You not give it as a perpetual gift
to the descendants of Abraham, Your
friend?

These descendants have dwelt in this land,
and they built in it a sanctuary to honor
You, saying:
"When we are faced with evil,
with the sword of judgment, or pestilence,
or famine,
we will stand before this house and before
You,
for this house is dedicated to You.
Then we will cry out to You in our affliction,
and You will listen to our plea and save us."

Observe how our enemies are now repaying
us
by coming to drive us out of the possession
You have given us.
O Lord, our God,
will You refuse to pass judgment on them?
We are powerless in the face of this vast
multitude
that is coming against us.
We do not know what to do;
therefore our eyes are turned toward You.

2 Chronicles 20:6-12

Prayer of David

Glory and honor are due to God alone

O Lord, God of Israel,
may You be blessed throughout eternity.
You, O Lord, possess grandeur and power
    to an infinite degree,
as well as majesty, splendor, and glory.
Everything in heaven and on earth is under
    Your dominion.
You, O Lord, have complete sovereignty;
You are exalted as King of all.
Riches and honor derive from You,
and You have dominion over all that exists.
You are the source of power and might;
grandeur and strength can be granted to
    anyone at Your discretion.

Therefore, our God, we give thanks to You,
and we offer praise to the majesty of Your
    Name.
We stand in Your presence as aliens;
we are merely Your guests, as was true of all
    our fathers;
our life on earth is nothing but a fleeting
    shadow that fades away.
I am well aware, O my God,
that You put hearts to the test
and that You rejoice when You observe an
    upright life.

O Lord, God of our fathers Abraham, Isaac,
and Jacob,
keep such thoughts in the hearts and minds
of Your people forever,
and direct their hearts toward You.

1 Chronicles 29:10-13, 15, 17a, 18

PRAYERS OF DEVOUT INDIVIDUALS

Prayer of Sarah and Tobiah
Marriage in God

Blessed are You, O God of our fathers;
may Your Name be praised throughout
eternity.
Let the heavens and Your entire creation
praise You for all ages.
You created Adam, and then You gave him
Eve
to afford him help and support;
from these two individuals the entire
human race descended.
You had decreed: "It is not good for the
man to be alone;
therefore We shall create for him a partner
like him."

Now, O Lord, You are fully aware that I
take this woman to be my wife
not as the result of lust,

but with an honorable end in mind.
Grant Your mercy to me and to her,
and permit us to live together to a happy
  advanced age.

Blessed are You, O God;
every holy and pure blessing derives from
  You.
May all Your chosen ones offer praise to You;
may they bless You forever.
Blessed are You, for You showed Your
  mercy
to two only children.
Grant [us] mercy, O Lord, and deliver [us];
may [our] lives achieve a full measure of
  happiness
through [our] mercy to others.

Tobit 8:5, 7, 15, 17

Prayer of Tobit

Praise of God Who afflicts only to heal

Blessed be the God of eternal life;
His Kingdom will endure throughout all
  ages.
The Lord scourges and then shows His
  mercy;
He brings up from the great abyss
those whom He casts down to the depths of
  the netherworld.

No one can escape His justice.

Praise the Lord, you Israelites, in the presence of the Gentiles,

for although He has dispersed you among them,

He has made manifest to you His greatness even there.

Exalt Him in the presence of every living being,

for He is the Lord our God,

our Father and our God for all eternity.

Even though He scourged you for your wicked deeds,

He will again show His mercy to all of you.

He will gather you together from the midst of the Gentiles

among whom you have been dispersed.

Once you return to Him with all your heart

and act in accordance with His Will,

then He will open His arms to you

and no longer conceal His face from you.

Hence reflect on what He has done for you

and exalt Him to the depths of your being.

Bless the Lord of righteousness

and praise the King of the ages.

In the land of my exile I exalt Him

and proclaim His power and majesty to a sinful nation:

"Repent, you sinners! Do what is right in
the Lord's sight!
If you do so, He may look with favor upon
you
and grant you His mercy.
As for me, I will exalt my God;
the King of heaven will be the source of my
joy.
Let all proclaim His majesty
and offer Him praise in Jerusalem."

Tobit 13:1-8

Prayer of Judith

Trust in God's Universal Providence

O my God,
please listen to the prayer of a widow.
You were the Author of former events
and of what preceded and followed them.
Moreover, what occurs in the present and
the future
has been authorized by You.
Whatever You devise comes into being;
the things You decide upon present themselves and say:
"Here we are!"

All Your plans await Your command,
and Your judgment derives from Your fore-
knowledge.

Your strength does not derive from num-
bers,
nor does Your power depend upon faithful
followers.
Rather, You are the God of the lowly
Who helps the oppressed and supports
those who are weak.
You are the Protector of those who are forsaken,
the Savior of those who are without any
hope.

Lord of heaven and earth,
Creator of the waters,
King of all You have created,
hear my prayer.
Let Your own people and all the tribes
clearly understand
that You are the God of power and might,
and that You are the only one
Who protects the people of Israel.

Judith 9:5-6, 11-12, 14

Prayer of Judith

Refuge in God's almighty power

Let the musical instruments sound forth;
offer a song to my God with tambourines,
chant to the Lord to the accompaniment of
cymbals.

Sing to Him a new refrain;
praise and exalt His Name.

I will sing a new hymn to my God.
O Lord, how majestic and glorious You are,
awesome in Your power and unable to be
surpassed.
Let all Your creatures serve You,
for You spoke and they came into existence.
When You sent forth Your Spirit, they were
created;
no one is able to resist Your Word.

Shaken to their foundations are the mountains as well as the seas,
and the rocks melt before Your glance like
wax.
Yet to those who fear You
You show endless mercy.

Judith 16:1, 13-15

Prayer of Mordecai

A plea for God's People

O Lord God, almighty King,
all things are subject to Your rule,
and there is no one who can thwart You
in Your determination to save Israel.
You created heaven and earth
and every marvelous thing that exists.

You are the Lord of all,
and no one can resist You.

Since You know all things, O Lord,
You are well aware
that it was not because of arrogance or
     pride or in a quest for glory
that I refused to bow down before Haman in
     his insolence.
I would not have hesitated to kiss the soles
     of his feet
if by doing so I could have ensured the sal-
     vation of Israel.
I merely acted in the manner I did
because I refused to place the honor of hu-
     mans above that of God.
I will not bow down before anyone
except You, O Lord.
It is not because of arrogant pride
that I am acting in this way.

And now, Lord God, our King, and God of
     Abraham,
I implore you to save Your people.
For our enemies are determined to elimi-
     nate us,
and their intention is to destroy the inheri-
     tance
that was Yours from the beginning.
Do not spurn Your people

whom You redeemed for Yourself out of
   Egypt.
Heed my entreaty;
take pity on Your inheritance,
and turn our sorrow into joy.
As a result we shall survive
to sing praise to Your Name, O Lord.

Esther C:1-10 (13:8-17)

Prayer of Esther

God alone has the power to save us

My Lord, our King,
You alone are our God.
Please help me, for I am alone
and I have no one else but You to turn to;
my life is in danger.
As a child I was always told
by the people of the land of my forefathers
that You, O Lord, chose Israel from among
   all peoples
and designated our fathers from among all
   their ancestors as a perpetual heritage,
and that all of Your promises to them were
   fulfilled.

Now, however, we have sinned in Your sight
   by worshiping the gods of our enemies,
and You have delivered us into their hands
because You are just, O Lord.

Some of our people now are rebelling
   against our condition of bitter servitude,
and they are determined to do away with
   the decree You have pronounced
and to destroy Your heritage
by silencing those who praise You
and extinguishing the glory of Your Temple
   and Your altar,
by joining with the pagans to acclaim their
   false gods
and to extol an earthly king forever.

O Lord, do not hand over Your scepter
to those who have rebelled against You.
Do not permit them to gloat over our down-
   fall,
but turn their own evil schemes against them
and make an example of our chief enemy.
Do not forget us, O Lord.
Be present to us in the time of our distress
and grant me courage, O King of gods and
   Ruler of every earthly power.

Grant me the wisdom to use persuasive
   words
so that our people may rise up against the
   enemy
and he and all those who are alive with him
   may perish.
Save us by Your power,

and come to my aid,
for I am alone
and have no one but You on whom to depend, O Lord.   Esther C:14-25 (14:4-9)

Prayer of Nehemiah

A plea for forgiveness and salvation

O Lord, God of heaven,
mighty and awesome God,
do not forsake Your Covenant of mercy
toward those who love You and keep Your
   Commandments.
May Your ears be attentive,
and Your eyes observant,
to look favorably upon the prayer that I,
   Your servant,
now offer in Your presence every night and
   day for Your servants the Israelites.

We admit the sins that we have committed
   against You,
sins concerning which I and my father's
   house are not without guilt.
We have offended You grievously
by not faithfully observing the Commandments, the statutes, and the ordinances
that You entrusted to Your servant Moses.
Despite this, please remember the promise
   You gave through Your servant Moses

when You said:
"Should you prove faithless,
I will scatter you among the nations.
But should you return to Me
and carefully observe My Commandments,
even though your people have been driven
to the farthest corners of the world,
I will assemble them from there
and return them to the place that I have
    designated
as the dwelling place for My Name."

These are Your servants, Your people,
whom You freed by Your awesome might
    and Your powerful hand.
O Lord, let Your ear be attentive to my
    prayer
and to the pleas of all Your servants who re-
    vere Your Name.
Grant victory to Your servant this day
and allow me to find favor with the king.

Nehemiah 1:5-11

PRAYERS OF THE SAGES

Prayer of Job

The living God Who vindicates

Would that my words were written down
and that they were inscribed for a perma-
    nent record,

cut in a rock forever
with an iron chisel and with lead.
But it is enough for me to know that my
　Savior lives,
and that upon the earth He will at last
　stand triumphant,
Whom I myself shall behold:
my own eyes, not those of another, shall
　gaze upon Him,
and in my mortal body I shall see God;
my being is consumed with longing to its
　innermost depths.

O Lord, I know that there is nothing beyond
　Your power,
and that no plan of Yours can fail to be ful-
　filled.
I have dealt with great things far beyond
　my understanding,
things too marvelous for me even to com-
　prehend.
I had heard of You from the reports of
　others,
but now my own eyes have beheld You.
Therefore, forgive me for what I have previ-
　ously said,
for which I repent in dust and ashes.

Job 19:23-26; 42:2-6

Prayer of the Sage for Wisdom

Lord, give me Wisdom

O God of my fathers, Lord of mercy,
You have created all things by Your mere
Word,
and in Your wisdom You designated man
to have dominion over the creatures of Your
handiwork,
to rule the world in holiness and justice,
and to render justice with unquestioned in-
tegrity.
Grant me Wisdom, the attendant at Your
throne,
and do not reject me from those numbered
among Your children.
For I am Your servant, the son of Your
handmaid,
someone who is weak and granted but a
short term of life,
and who is also lacking in the ability to render fair judgment
and to comprehend laws.

Indeed, even if some should achieve perfection among the human race,
but Wisdom, who derives from You, is not
with them,
they shall be regarded as persons of no es-
teem.

In Your presence is Wisdom who knows
Your works
and was there when You created the world,
who comprehends what is pleasing to You
and what is in conformity with Your commands.

Send Wisdom forth from Your holy heavens
and from Your throne of glory entrust me to
her guidance,
so that she may be with me and work with
me,
in order that I may know what is Your Will
in my regard.
Wisdom knows and comprehends all things,
and she will guide me carefully in my actions
and safeguard me by her power.

Wisdom 9:1-6, 9-11

Prayer of the Sage for Trust in God's Word

The Lord nourished His people with the food of Angels

O Lord, You nourished Your people with
the food of Angels
and provided them with an unending sup-
ply of bread from heaven
that they had not toiled for,

endowed with every possible delight and
pleasing to every taste.

For this gift of Yours revealed the depth
of Your feelings toward Your children,
and, sating the desire of those who received
it,
was adapted to the preferred taste of each
person,
so that Your children whom You loved
would learn, O Lord,
that it is not the various kinds of foods that
nourish humans,
but that it is Your Word that preserves
those who believe You.
For Your judgments are magnificent, almost
beyond description.

Wisdom 16:20-21, 26; 17:la

Prayer of Sirach

Prayer of entreaty for the holy city, Jerusalem

C ome to our assistance, O Lord of the uni-
verse,
and let all the nations be in dread of You.
Raise Your hand against the pagans
so that they may come to recognize Your
power.
You have previously used us to show them
Your holiness;
now use them to reveal to us Your glory.

Thus they will come to know, as we already
  know,
that there is no other God but You.

Offer new signs and work new wonders;
exhibit the splendor of Your right hand and
  arm.
Gather together all the tribes of Jacob
so that they may inherit the land as in for-
  mer times.
Show mercy to the people who bear Your
  Name,
Israel, whom You designated as Your first-
  born.
Have pity on Your holy city,
Jerusalem, where You dwell.
Let Zion be filled with Your majesty,
Your Temple with Your glory.

Sirach 36:1-5, 10-13

Prayer of Sirach in Gratitude

Prayer of thanksgiving for God's help

I give You thanks, O God of my father;
I offer You praise, O God my Savior.
I will make Your Name known, for You
  have been my life's refuge;
You have been ready to help me against my
  foes.
You have rescued me when I was faced with
  death

and raised my body from the pit.
From the grasp of the netherworld
You have snatched away my feet.

I turned in every direction but no one offered to help me;
I looked for someone to support me but I was unable to find anyone.
But then I recalled how merciful the Lord had been,
His acts of kindness to all preceding generations.
For He extends a saving hand to those who seek to take refuge in Him
and rescues them from whatever evils threaten them.

Therefore I raised my voice from the depths of the earth,
from the gates of the netherworld my plea came forth,
as I poured forth my request:
O Lord, You are my Father,
You are my defender and my Savior.
Do not abandon me in this sea of troubles,
in the midst of storms and perils.
I will never cease to praise Your Name
or to be faithful in my prayers to You.

Thereupon the Lord heard my cry
and gave ear to my appeal.

He preserved me from every kind of evil
and saved me in my time of trouble.

For this reason I thank Him and I offer
  Him praise;
I bless the Name of the Lord.   Sirach 51:1-2, 7-12

PRAYERS OF THE PROPHETS

Prayer of Isaiah in Thanksgiving

Joy of God's ransomed people

I offer You thanks, O Lord;
although I have aroused Your anger,
that anger has abated, and You have offered
  me Your consolation.
God is truly my Savior;
I am confident and without fear.
The Lord is the source of my strength and
  my courage;
He has been my Savior.

Joyfully you will draw water
at the fountain of salvation,
and on that day you will say:
Offer thanks to the Lord and glorify His
  Name;
among all nations proclaim His deeds,
show forth how exalted is His Name.
Sing praise to the Lord for His glorious deeds;

let these be acclaimed throughout all the
    earth.
Shout with joy, O city of Zion,
for triumphant in your midst
is the Holy One of Israel.   Isaiah 12:1-6

Prayer of Isaiah for God's Judgment

The Divine Vindicator

We have been blessed with a strong city;
the Lord has established walls and ramparts
    to protect us.
Throw open the gates
to allow entrance to a nation that is just
whose word is worthy of trust.
You grant peace to a nation of firm purpose;
peace is its reward for its trust in You.
Have trust in the Lord forever,
for He will be our Rock forever.

The just travel along a smooth road;
the path of the just You have made level.
For the path You wish us to follow and
    Your judgments, O Lord,
we look to You.
Your Name and Your title
are our souls' desire.
My soul yearns for Your presence during
    the night;
yes, my innermost spirit keeps vigil for You.

When the earth encounters the dawn of
   Your judgment,
those who dwell there will comprehend the
   meaning of justice.
O Lord, You are the source of our peace,
for You have accomplished everything we
   have done.   Isaiah 26:1-4, 7-9, 12

Prayer of Isaiah for Trust in God

Prayer of trust in need

O Lord, have pity on us who wait for You;
be our strength each morning
and our salvation in difficult situations.
At a roaring sound people will flee;
when You rise in Your majesty, nations dis-
   perse.
People gather up spoil the way caterpillars
   are gathered up;
they seize upon it like an onrush of locusts.

Exalt the Lord Who is enthroned on high;
He fills Zion with justice and a sense of
   righteousness.
That which causes Zion to endure,
the riches that preserve her, are wisdom and
   knowledge;
her treasure is the fear of the Lord. . . .

The highways have been left desolate;
travelers have abandoned the paths.

Covenants are broken and their provisions
   ignored—
yet no one gives it a thought.

The country is desolate in mourning,
Lebanon cringes with shame. . . .
Now I will rise up, says the Lord;
now is the time for Me to be exalted, to be
   lifted up.   Isaiah 33:2-10

Prayer of Hezekiah

Prayer in time of sickness

O n one occasion I said:
"At the midpoint of my life I must depart.
I shall be carried to the gates of the netherworld
for my remaining years."
I said: "I shall behold the Lord no longer
in the land of the living.
No longer shall I encounter other humans
among those who inhabit the earth."
My dwelling, like the tent of a shepherd,
has been struck down and carried away
   from my sight.
You have brought my life to an end,
like a weaver who cuts away the final thread.

Day and night You allow me to be in torment;
my cries resound until the break of dawn.

Like a lion You mangle all my bones;
day and night You allow me to be in torment.
Like a swallow I emit shrill cries;
I moan in the manner of a dove.
My eyes grow weak as I gaze toward
heaven.
O Lord, I am in a difficult situation; be my
salvation.

What am I to say? What can I tell Him?
He has so determined it.
I shall continue to endure through all my
years
despite my bitterness of soul.
Those people live who are protected by the
Lord;
You are the source of the life of my spirit.
You have granted me health and life;
thus has my bitterness been transformed
into a peaceful outlook.

You preserved my life from the pit of destruction
when You chose to forgive all my sins.

For just as the netherworld does not give
You thanks,
nor does death praise You,
so neither do those who descend into the pit
expect Your mercy.
It is the living who give You thanks,

as I do today.
Fathers make known to their sons
Your faithfulness, O God.

The Lord is our Savior;
accompanied by stringed instruments we
    shall sing
in the house of the Lord
all the days of our life.   Isaiah 38:10-20

Prayer of Jeremiah

The lament of the people in war and famine

Let my eyes flow with tears
day and night, without ceasing,
over the immense destruction that has over-
    whelmed
the virgin daughter of my people,
bestowing an incurable wound.
If I walk out into the field,
I behold those who have been slain by the
    sword.
If I enter the city,
I see those who are consumed by hunger.
Even prophets and priests
search for food in a land they no longer know.

Have You forsaken Judah completely?
Is Zion now loathsome in Your sight?
Why have You dealt us a blow
that is not able to be healed?

We wait for a time of peace, but to no avail;
we pray for a period of healing, yet terror
   comes instead.
We confess, O Lord, our wickedness
and the guilt incurred by our ancestors;
we admit that we have sinned against You.

For Your Name's sake do not turn aside
   from us;
do not allow the throne of Your glory to
   incur disgrace;
remember Your Covenant with us and do
   not forsake it.   Jeremiah 14:17-21

Prayer of an Unknown Prophet

A prayer in time of great distress

D o not forget, O Lord, what misfortune
   has overtaken us;
look upon us and realize our disgrace.
The lands of our inheritance have been
   turned over to strangers,
our homes to foreigners.
We have become orphans, without fathers;
our mothers are now widowed.
We are forced to purchase the water we drink,
we must buy our own wood.

The yokes of those who drive us strangle
   our necks;
we are exhausted but allowed no time to
   rest. . . .

Our ancestors, who sinned, have now all
   died,
but we continue to bear their guilt.
There is no longer joy in our hearts;
where we once danced, now we mourn.
Our heads are no longer adorned with gar-
   lands;
wretchedness has befallen us, for we have
   sinned.
Our hearts are sick about this situation;
the mere thought of it causes our eyes to
   grow dim.

You, O Lord, will reign forever;
Your throne stands invincible from age to age.
Why, then, have You forgotten us
and abandoned us for so long a time?
Lead us back to You, O Lord, so that we
   may be restored to Your friendship;
give us once again such days as we formerly
   experienced.   Lamentations 5:1-7, 15-17, 19-21

Prayer of Baruch

A plea for forgiveness and salvation

Lord Almighty, God of Israel,
the weary and the distraught call upon You.
Hear our prayer, O Lord, for You are a merciful God;
forgive us who have sinned against You.

For Your throne is everlasting,
while we continue to perish.
Lord Almighty, God of Israel,
hear the prayer of Israel's remnant,
the descendants of those who sinned against
    You.
Since they did not live in accordance with
    the Law of the Lord, their God,
the effects of their sins still afflict us.

Do not keep in mind at this time the mis-
    deeds of our ancestors,
but remain faithful to Your own Name and
    the works of Your hand.
For You are the Lord our God,
and to You, O Lord, we will offer praise.
You instilled into our hearts the fear of You
so that we may call upon Your Name
and praise You during our captivity,
until we have removed from our hearts
every trace of the wickedness of our ances-
    tors who sinned against You.

Baruch 3:1-7

Prayer of Azariah

Trust in God's power for deliverance

Blessed are You and worthy of praise,
O Lord, the God of our fathers.
Your Name will be glorious forever.

For You have shown justice in everything
  You have done;
all Your deeds are beyond reproach, all
  Your paths are straight,
and all Your judgments are correct.
We confess that we have sinned and broken
  Your laws
by departing from Your path,
and there is no kind of evil that we have not
  perpetrated.
To preserve the honor of Your Name do not
  deliver us up forever
or deprive us of Your Covenant.

Do not deprive us of Your mercy,
for the sake of Abraham, Your beloved,
Isaac Your servant, and Jacob Your holy one,
to whom You promised to make their off-
  spring
as numerous as the stars of the heavens
or the sand on the seashore.
For we have suffered, O Lord, more than
  any other nation,
and we are subjugated everywhere in the
  world today
as the result of our sinfulness.
In our time we have no prince, prophet, or
  leader,
no holocaust, sacrifice, sacred offering, or
  incense,

no place to offer firstfruits, to seek Your
favor.

But with a repentant heart and in a spirit of
humility
let us be welcomed.
As though we were offering holocausts of
rams and bulls
or thousands of healthy lambs,
so regard our sacrifice in Your presence this
day
as we follow You unquestioningly,
for those who trust in You cannot be made
to feel ashamed.
From this moment we will follow You with
our whole heart;
we will fear You and pray to You.

Daniel 3:26, 27, 29, 34-41

Doxological Prayer of the Three Young Men

Let all creatures praise the Lord

Blessed are You, O Lord, the God of our
ancestors,
worthy of praise and glory forever.
Blessed is Your holy and glorious Name,
worthy of praise and glory forever.
Blessed are You in the Temple of Your holy
glory,

worthy of praise and glory forever.
Blessed are You on the throne of Your king-
    dom,
worthy of praise and glory forever.
Blessed are You Who behold the depths
from Your throne upon the cherubim,
worthy of praise and glory forever.
Blessed are You in the firmament of heaven,
worthy of praise and glory forever.

Bless the Lord, all you works of the Lord;
praise and exalt Him forever.
Angels of the Lord, bless the Lord;
praise and exalt Him forever.
You heavens, bless the Lord;
praise and exalt Him forever.
All you waters above the heavens, bless the
    Lord;
praise and exalt Him forever.
All you powers of the Lord, bless the Lord;
praise and exalt Him forever.
Sun and moon, bless the Lord;
praise and exalt Him forever.
Stars of heaven, bless the Lord;
praise and exalt Him forever.

All rain and dew, bless the Lord;
praise and exalt Him forever.
All you winds, bless the Lord;
praise and exalt Him forever.

Fire and heat, bless the Lord;
praise and exalt Him forever.
Winter cold and summer heat, bless the
   Lord;
praise and exalt Him forever.
Dew and rain, bless the Lord;
praise and exalt Him forever.
Frost and chill, bless the Lord;
praise and exalt Him forever.
Ice and snow, bless the Lord;
praise and exalt Him forever.
Nights and days, bless the Lord;
praise and exalt Him forever.
Light and darkness, bless the Lord;
praise and exalt Him forever.
Lightning and clouds, bless the Lord;
praise and exalt Him forever.

Let the earth bless the Lord;
praise and exalt Him forever.
Mountains and hills, bless the Lord;
praise and exalt Him forever.
Every plant that grows, bless the Lord;
praise and exalt Him forever.
Springs of water, bless the Lord;
praise and exalt Him forever.
Seas and rivers, bless the Lord;
praise and exalt Him forever.
Dolphins and all creatures that live in
   water, bless the Lord;

praise and exalt Him forever.
Every kind of bird, bless the Lord;
praise and exalt Him forever.
All animals, wild and tame, bless the Lord;
praise and exalt Him forever.

All the human race, bless the Lord;
praise and exalt Him forever.
O Israel, bless the Lord;
praise and exalt Him forever.
You priests of the Lord, bless the Lord;
praise and exalt Him forever.
You servants of the Lord, bless the Lord;
praise and exalt Him forever.
Spirits and souls of the just, bless the Lord;
praise and exalt Him forever.
You who are holy and humble in heart,
    bless the Lord;
praise and exalt Him forever.

Hananiah, Azariah, and Mishael, bless the
    Lord;
praise and exalt Him forever.
For He has rescued us from Hades
and saved us from the power of death.
He has liberated us from the fiery furnace,
and from the fire He has delivered us.
Give thanks to the Lord, for He is good,
for His mercy endures forever.

Bless the God of gods, all you who fear the
    Lord;
praise Him and give thanks to Him
for His mercy endures forever.

Daniel 3:52-90

Prayer of Daniel for God's Pardon

An appeal to God's merciful Covenant

O Lord, great and awesome God,
You maintain Your Covenant of mercy
toward those who love You and keep Your
    Commandments.
We have sinned, engaged in wickedness,
    and done evil deeds;
we have rebelled against You and broken
    Your Commandments and Your laws.
We have refused to obey Your servants, the
    Prophets
who announced Your message
to our kings, our princes, our ancestors,
and all the people of the land.

Justice, O Lord, is Your hallmark;
we are filled with shame even to this day—
the inhabitants of Judah, the residents of
    Jerusalem,
and all the people of Israel, near and far,
throughout the countries to which You have
    scattered them
because of their treachery to You.

O Lord, like our kings, our princes, and our ancestors,
we are filled with shame that we have sinned against You.
But You, O Lord, our God,
are filled with compassion and forgiveness.
Despite that, we rebelled against You
and ignored Your command, O Lord, our God,
that we were to live by the Law You gave us
through Your servants the Prophets.

Because all Israel disobeyed Your Law and went astray,
paying no heed to Your commands,
the promised retribution recorded in the Law of Moses, the servant of God,
was inflicted upon us for our sins.
You, O Lord, our God, acted justly in doing what You did,
for we did not listen to what You had commanded.
But then, O Lord, our God,
You led Your people out of the land of Egypt with a strong hand
and established Your Name even to this day.

We have sinned,
and we admit our guilt.

O Lord, in accordance with all Your just
  deeds,
turn away Your anger and Your wrath from
  Your city Jerusalem.
Listen, therefore, O God,
to the prayer and petition of Your servant,
and, for the sake of Your glory,
show Your abundant mercy to Your desolate sanctuary.

I beg You, O my God, to pay heed and listen;
let Your eyes behold the destruction that
  has befallen
the city that bears Your Name.
We offer our petition to You,
relying not on our just deeds
but on Your inexhaustible mercy.
O Lord, listen to us!
O Lord, grant us pardon!
O Lord, be attentive to our plea and act
  without any delay
for Your own sake, O my God,
because this city and Your people bear Your
  Name!   Daniel 9:4-11, 14-19

Prayer of Jonah

Psalm of thanksgiving

In my distress I cried out to the Lord,
and He answered my prayer.

From the midst of the netherworld I begged
    for help,
and You heard my voice.
For You hurled me into the deep, into the
    midst of the sea,
and the flood waters enveloped me;
beneath all Your breakers and Your billows
I was submerged.

Then I said: "I have been exiled from Your
    sight.
Never again will I gaze upon Your holy
    Temple."
The waters swirled around me, endangering
    my life;
I was enveloped by the abyss
as seaweed clung to my body.
Down I descended to the base of the moun-
    tains;
the gates of the netherworld were closing
    behind me forever.
But You rescued my life from the pit,
O Lord, my God.

When my soul grew faint within me,
I remembered the Lord.
You heard my prayer
in Your sacred Temple.
Those who worship worthless idols
renounce the source of their mercy.

But I, with jubilant praise,
will offer sacrifice to You.
The vows that I have made I will keep,
for deliverance is from the Lord.

Jonah 2:3-10

Prayer of Micah

Cry for help in time of affliction

O Lord, use Your staff to shepherd Your
  people,
the flock of Your inheritance
that grazes separately in a woodland,
in the midst of Carmel.
Let them be fed in Bashan and Gilead,
as in the days of old.
As happened in those days when You led us
  forth from the land of Egypt,
show us marvelous signs.

The nations shall behold Your works and be
  put to shame
despite all their power.
Their hands shall be placed over their
  mouths;
their ears shall be unable to hear.
They shall grovel in the dust like serpents,
like reptiles on the ground.
They shall emerge fearfully from their hid-
  ing places,

trembling with fear of You, O Lord, our
God.

Who can equal You, the God Who pardons
guilt
and forgives the sins of those who remain
from His inheritance,
Who does not persist forever in His anger,
but rather takes delight in showing
clemency,
and Who will once again have compassion
on us,
casting aside our guilt?

You will hurl all our sins
into the depths of the sea.
You will show Your fidelity to Jacob
and Your mercy to Abraham,
as You have sworn to our ancestors from
ancient times.   Micah 7:14-20

Prayer of Habakkuk

God comes to judge

O Lord, Your renown has not been hidden
from me,
and I feared, O Lord, the actions You might
decide upon.
In the course of the years restore that
renown;

over a period of time make it known once
   again;
in Your wrath do not neglect to show Your
   compassion.

You have come forth to save Your people,
to rescue Your anointed one.
Decay afflicts my bones,
and my legs tremble beneath the weight of
   my body.
I look forward to the day of distress
that will come upon those who attack us.

For even though the fig tree fails to blossom
and no fruit is on the vines,
though the olive tree brings forth no leaves
and the vineyards produce no nourishment,
though the flocks escape from the fold
and no herd can be found in the stalls,
yet I will rejoice in the Lord
and exult in God my Savior.

The Lord my God is the source of my
   strength;
He makes my feet as swift as those of the
   deer
and enables me to ascend the heights.

Habakkuk 3:2, 13a, 16b-19

THE PSALMS—PRAYERBOOK OF THE HOLY SPIRIT

The Psalms may be looked upon as the prayerbook of the Holy Spirit. Over the long centuries of Israel's existence, the Spirit of God inspired the psalmists (typified by David) to compose magnificent prayers and hymns for every religious desire and need, mood and feeling. Thus, the Psalms have great power to raise minds to God, to inspire devotion, to evoke gratitude in favorable times, and to bring consolation and strength in times of trial.

THE PSALMS:
PRAYER OF THE ASSEMBLY

*T*HE Psalms are the prayer of God's assembly, the public prayer par excellence of the People of God. No prayer of Israel is comparable to the Psalter because of its universal character. The idea of the unity of the chosen people's prayer guided its elaboration as well as its adoption by the Church.

In giving us the Psalter, which sums up the major aspects of our relationship to our Creator and Redeemer, God puts into our mouths the words He wishes to hear, and indicates to us the dimensions of prayer.

"The Psalms recall to mind the truths revealed by God to the chosen people, which were at one time frightening and at another filled with wonderful tenderness; they keep repeating and fostering the hope of the promised Redeemer which in ancient times was kept alive with song, either around the hearth or in the stately temple; they show forth in splendid light the prophesied glory of Jesus Christ: first, His supreme and eternal power, then His lowly coming to this earthly exile, His kingly dignity and priestly power, and finally His beneficent labors, and the shedding of His Blood for our redemption.

"In a similar way they express the joy, the bitterness, the hope and fear of our hearts and our desire of loving God and hoping in Him alone, and our mystic ascent to divine tabernacles" (Pope Pius XII, *Mediator Dei*, no. 148).

In short, the Psalms constitute an inexhaustible treasury of prayers for every occasion and mood in a format that is true to the whole tradition of the History of Salvation.

Prayer for True Happiness

The way of the just

Happy are those who refuse to follow
the advice of the wicked.
They do not walk along the path of sinners
or associate with the insolent.
Rather, they delight in the Law of the Lord
and meditate on it in all their waking hours.

Such persons are like a tree
planted near a running stream
that yields its fruit when its season arrives,
and whose leaves remain verdant.
They succeed in whatever they do.

This is not true of the wicked, not to the
slightest degree;
they are like chaff driven away by the wind.
Therefore at the judgment the wicked shall
not stand,
nor shall sinners, in the assembly of the just.
For the Lord guards carefully the way of the
just,
but the way of the wicked disappears.

Psalm 1

Prayer of Trust in God

A call for God's help

When I call upon You, answer me, O my
just God,

You Who offer me solace in distress;
have pity on me, and listen to my prayer.

Sinner, repent

O you of worldly rank, how long will You
continue to be obtuse?
Why do you cherish what is of no value and
pursue worthless goals?
Remember that the Lord does marvelous
things for His faithful ones;
the Lord will not turn a deaf ear to me when
I call upon Him.
Be fearful and do not sin;
reflect in silence as you lie upon your beds.
Offer worthy sacrifices
and have trust in the Lord.

Confidence in God

Many complain: "Oh, if only we could experience better times!"
O Lord, allow the light of Your countenance
to shine upon us.
From You I receive more gladness in my
heart
than when I have a surplus of grain and
wine.
No sooner do I lie down than I fall asleep
peacefully,
for You alone, O Lord,
afford security to my dwelling.   Psalm 4

Prayer for Divine Assistance

A call for help

Pay heed to my words, O Lord;
attend to my sighs.
Give heed to my call for help,
my King and my God.
To You I offer my prayer, O Lord;
at dawn You hear my voice;
at dawn I bring my petition expectantly before You.

Hatred of evil

For You, O God, take no delight in wickedness;
no evil person remains in Your presence;
the arrogant are not permitted to stand in
Your sight.
You loathe all evildoers;
You destroy all who swear falsely.
Those who are bloodthirsty and deceitful
are abhorred by the Lord.

Guidance

But because of Your gracious kindness
I will enter Your house.
I will worship at Your sacred Temple
with a holy fear of You, O Lord.
So that I may withstand my enemies,
guide me in the paths of Your justice;
guide me along Your way.

Destruction of the wicked

For from their mouth no sincere word
  comes forth;
their heart is filled with plans for treachery.
Their throat serves as an open grave;
they use their tongue for flattery.
Inflict punishment on them, O God;
let them fall as a result of their treachery.
Cast them out because of their manifold offenses,
for they have acted in rebellion against You.

Protection of the just

However, grant that all who take refuge in
  You
will be glad and exult forever.
Offer them Your protection,
so that You may be the source of the joy
of those who love Your Name.
For You, O Lord, shower Your blessings
  upon the just;
You protect the just with the shield of Your
  mercy.   Psalm 5

Prayer of Repentance

Sorrow for sin

O Lord, do not reprove me in Your anger
or chastise me in Your wrath.

Have pity on me, O Lord, for I am suffering
  affliction;
heal me, O Lord, for my body quivers in terror.
My soul, too, is completely frightened;
how long will You keep me waiting, O
  Lord?

The mercy of God

Come to me, O Lord, and preserve my life;
save me because of Your kindness.
For not one person among the dead remem-
  bers You;
in the netherworld who offers You thanks?
I am exhausted with my sighing;
every night I flood my bed with tears;
my couch is drenched because of my weeping.
My eyes have grown dim with sorrow;
they have become aged by all my enemies.

Confidence in prayer

Depart from my presence, all you evildoers,
for the Lord has paid heed to the sound of
  my weeping.
The Lord has heard my prayer;
the Lord has accepted my petition.
All of my enemies shall be put to shame because of their utter terror;
they shall retreat in utter shame.   Psalm 6

Prayer in Time of Trouble

Plea for God's help

O Lord, my God, in You I seek refuge;
keep me safe from all my pursuers and res-
    cue me,
lest I become like the prey of a lion,
ready to be torn to pieces, with no one to
    come to my aid.

Cry of innocence

O Lord, my God, if I have any fault in this,
if there is some guilt on my part,
if I have repaid friendship with treachery,
I who spared the lives of those who for no
    justifiable reason were my foes—
let my enemies pursue and overtake me;
let them trample my life to the ground
and crush my glory in the dust.

Appeal to God's judgment

Rise up, O Lord, in Your wrath;
take action against the fury of my enemies;
fulfill the judgment You have decreed.
Let the assemblage of all the peoples sur-
    round You;
be enthroned on high above them.
The Lord passes judgment on the nations.
Grant me justice, O Lord, because I am just
and because of my innocence.

Let the malice of the wicked be extin-
  guished,
but continue to sustain the just,
O searcher of heart and soul, O just God.

Psalm 7:1-10

Prayer Extolling the Majesty of God and the Dignity of Humans

Finite nature and infinite majesty

O Lord our God,
how glorious is Your Name throughout all
  the earth.
Your majesty has been exalted above the
  heavens.
Out of the mouths of newborn babes and in-
  fants
You have fashioned praise to silence Your
  foes
and to shame those who are hostile and
  seeking revenge.
When I behold Your heavens, the work of
  Your hands,
the moon and the stars in the firmament
  You established—
what are humans that You should remember them,
mere mortals that You should be concerned
  about their destiny?

Humans accorded dignity and power by God

You have made them only slightly less than
the Angels
and given them a crown of glory and honor.
You have appointed them to rule over the
works of Your hands,
placing all of Your creation under their dominion:
all sheep and oxen,
as well as the beasts of the field,
the birds of the air, the fish of the sea,
and whatever swims in the waters You have
given us.
O Lord, our Lord,
Your Name is truly glorious throughout all
the earth.   Psalm 8

Prayer to God the Supreme Good

The Lord is my portion

I bless the Lord Who is my counselor;
even during the night my heart encourages
me toward the good.
I have the Lord ever before my eyes;
with Him at my right hand I shall never be
afraid.
Therefore my heart is filled with gladness
and my soul rejoices;
my body, too, is filled with confidence,

because You will not dispatch my soul to
the netherworld,
nor will You allow Your faithful one to suffer corruption.

Joyous resurrection

You will show me the path to eternal life,
the fullness of joys to be experienced in
Your presence,
the delights to be found at Your right hand
forever.

Psalm 16:7-11

Praise of God the Lawgiver

Perfection of God's Law

The Law of the Lord is flawless,
affording refreshment to the soul.
The decrees of the Lord are worthy of trust,
for they endow the uneducated with wisdom.
The precepts of the Lord are truly just,
causing the heart to rejoice.
The commands of the Lord are easily com-
prehended,
enlightening the mind.
The fear of the Lord is a virtue
that must endure forever.
The ordinances of the Lord are flawless,
and all of them are just.

They are even more precious than gold,
than a mass of the purest gold;
they are also sweeter than syrup
or honey from the hive.
Though Your servant is careful to observe
them
and truly diligent in keeping them,
yet some failings can pass unnoticed.
Cleanse me from my faults of which I am
unaware.
From unbridled sin especially, preserve
Your servant;
let it not gain power over me.
Then I shall be blameless
and innocent of serious sin.
Let the words of my mouth and the
thoughts of my heart
find favor before You,
O Lord, my Rock and my Redeemer.

Psalm 19:8-15

Prayer of Christ on the Cross

Lament in suffering

My God, My God, why have You forsaken
Me?
Why are You far removed from My prayer,
from the words of My petition?
O My God, I cry out to You during the day
and You do not answer Me,

at night and no relief is offered Me.

Yet You are enthroned in the sacred place,
O glory of Israel.

In You our ancestors placed their trust;

they trusted, and You gave them deliverance.

When they cried out to You, You enabled
them to escape;

they trusted in You, and they were not put
to shame.

But I am more of a worm than a human
being;

I am scorned by men, despised by the people.

All who see Me deride Me;

they mock Me with sneering lips, they shake
their heads:

"He relied on the Lord; let the Lord deliver
Him,

let the Lord rescue Him if He loves Him."

You have guided Me since I was first
formed;

You provided Me with security at My
mother's breast.

To You I was committed at birth;

from My emergence from My mother's
womb You have been My God.

Stay not far from Me, for I am in distress;

be ever near, for there is no one else on
whom I can depend for help.

Joy of the risen Savior

I will proclaim Your Name to My brethren;
in the midst of the assembly I will offer You
praise:

"Those of you who fear the Lord, praise
Him!
All you descendants of Jacob, give Him
glory!
Revere Him, all you descendants of Israel!
For He has not spurned or disregarded
the wretched in their suffering,
nor did He turn His face away from them,
but when they cried out to Him, He heard
them."
Therefore I will offer praise for His kindness in the vast assembly;
I will fulfill My vows in the presence of
those who fear Him.
Those who are lowly shall eat their fill;
those who seek the Lord shall praise Him:
"May your hearts be ever filled with joy."

Psalm 22:2-12, 23-27

Prayer to the Good Shepherd

Constant protector

The Lord is my shepherd; I shall not lack
for any good thing.
In verdant pastures He grants me rest.

Beside restful waters He leads me;
He invigorates my soul.
He directs me in paths of righteousness
so that His Name may be glorified.
Even though I wander through a dark valley
I will fear no evil;
for You are at my side
with Your rod and Your staff
that fill me with courage.

Considerate host

You spread a table before me
as my foes look on.
You anoint my head with oil;
my cup is filled to overflowing.
Only goodness and kindness will be my
    companions
every day of my life.
And I shall establish my dwelling in the
    house of the Lord
forever and ever.   Psalm 23

Prayer in Time of Fear

Trust in God

The Lord is the source of my light and my
    salvation;
whom should I fear?
The Lord is my life's place of refuge;

of whom shall I be frightened?
When evildoers rush toward me
to consume my flesh,
my attackers and my foes
themselves trip and fall to the ground.
Even if an army should encamp against me,
I will not fear in my heart.
Even if war should be waged against me,
even then I will not cease to have hope.

Secure refuge

There is only one thing I ask of the Lord;
this is what I seek:
that I may dwell in the house of the Lord
as long as I live,
that I may behold the loveliness of the Lord
and meditate on His Temple.
For the Lord will conceal me in His abode
when the day of trouble arrives.
He will conceal me in the sanctuary of His
tent;
He will place me high upon a rock.
Even now I hold my head high
above my enemies who surround me on
every side.
And in His tent I will offer sacrifices
with cries of gladness.
I will sing chants of praise to the Lord.

Psalm 27:1-6

Prayer for God's Mercy

Hope of the penitent

O Lord, do not punish me in Your anger;
do not chastise me in Your wrath.
For Your arrows have pierced deeply into
my flesh,
and Your judgment has come down upon
me.
My flesh has become emaciated because of
Your anger;
my bones have become weak because of my
sins.
For my sinful deeds have overwhelmed me;
they are a heavy burden, far beyond my en-
durance.

Sorrow for sin

I am at the point of exhaustion,
and I am unable to overcome my grief.
Indeed, I acknowledge my sinfulness;
I mourn my guilt.
But those who are my enemies without just
cause are strong;
many have become my foes for no good reason.
Those who repay good deeds with evil
taunt me for following a righteous path.
Do not abandon me, O Lord;
my God, remain close to me.

Hasten to my aid, O Lord,
You Who are my salvation.   Psalm 38:1-5, 18-23

Prayer of Longing and Hope

Longing to see God

A s a deer longs for running waters,
so my soul yearns for You, O God.
My soul thirsts for God, the living God.
When shall I be allowed to behold the face
   of God?
My tears are my nourishment day and night
as people sneer at me day after day, saying:
"Where is your God?"
Now that I am unburdening my soul
I recall those times
when I journeyed with the throng
as I led them in procession to the house of
   God,
to the accompaniment of loud cries of joy
   and thanksgiving,
with the multitude joyfully participating.
Why are you so grief-stricken, O my soul?
Why do your sighs arise within me?
Have trust in God.
For I shall once again be expressing my
   gratitude to Him
when I am in the presence of my Savior and
   my God.

Hopeful of God's promises

Since my soul is troubled within me,
I will remember You
from the land of the Jordan and of Hermon,
from Mount Misar.
The depths of the sea resound
in the roar of Your waterfalls.
All Your waves and Your surf
cascade over me.
During the day the Lord bestows His grace,
and at night I rejoice in His song,
a prayer-offering to my living God.
I sing to God, my Rock:
"Why have You forgotten me?
Why am I forced to wander about in
  mourning
while my enemies oppress me?"
It crushes my spirit that my foes taunt me
as they jeer at me day after day, saying:
  "Where is your God?"
Why are you so grief-stricken, O my soul?
Why do your sighs arise within me?
Have trust in God!
For I shall once again be expressing my
  gratitude to Him
when I am in the presence of my Savior and
  my God.

Psalm 42:2-12

Prayer of Longing for God

Plea to enter God's dwelling

Show me Your justice, O God, and take up
  Your sword for me
to contend against a faithless people;
from liars and evil persons rescue me.
For You, O God, are the source of my
  strength.
Why do You remain so far away from me?
Why am I forced to wander about in
  mourning
while my enemies oppress me?
Pour forth Your light and Your faithfulness;
they shall serve a a beacon
and lead me to Your holy mountain,
to the place of Your dwelling.
Then will I enter the sanctuary of God,
the God Who is the source of my happiness
  and joy.
Then I will express my thanks upon the
  harp to You,
O God, my God.

Hope in God

Why are you so grief-stricken, O my soul?
Why do your sighs arise within me?
Have trust in God!
For I shall once again be expressing my
  gratitude to Him

when I am in the presence of my Savior and
my God.   Psalm 43

Prayer before Confession

Sincere sorrow for sin

Show mercy to me, O God, in Your goodness;
as a sign of Your great compassion wipe out
my offenses.
Cleanse me completely from my guilt
and grant me forgiveness of my sins.
For I acknowledge that I have sinned,
and the realization of that fact is constantly
on my mind.
Against You only have I acted sinfully
and perpetrated what is evil in Your eyes.
Thus You are justified in Your sentence
and will be vindicated when You condemn.
In truth, I came forth into this world in a
state of guilt,
and my mother conceived me in sin.
I know that You are pleased with a sincere
heart,
and in my innermost heart You instruct me
in wisdom.
A clean heart grant to me, O God,
and revive a steadfast spirit within me.
Do not cast me out from Your presence
nor deprive me of Your Holy Spirit.

Let me once again experience the joy of
Your saving grace,
and a subservient spirit sustain in me.

Praise of God for His mercy

I will instruct sinners in Your ways,
and those who have fallen shall return to
You.
Do not permit me to be guilty of shedding
another's blood, O God, my saving God;
then I shall revel in Your justice.
O Lord, loosen my lips,
and my mouth shall shout Your praise.
For sacrifices are not pleasing to You;
if I were to offer a holocaust, You would not
accept it.
My sacrifice, O God, is a spirit filled with
contrition.
O God, You will not spurn a heart that is
contrite and humble.   Psalm 51:3-8, 12-19

Prayer To End Wars

Fortify us against enemies

O God, You have turned away from us and
shattered our defenses;
although we have roused Your anger, please
come to our aid.
You have shaken the country and split it
apart;

seal its cracks, for it is crumbling.
You have allowed Your people to suffer
    hardships;
You have given us wine that stupefies our
    senses.
You have offered those who fear You a refuge
to which they may flee and escape injury.
So that Your loved ones may find shelter,
help us by the power of Your right hand
    and answer our prayer.

Lead us to victory

Who will lead me into the fortified city?
Who will direct me into Edom?
It appears, O Lord, that You have rejected
    us,
and that You will not march forth, O God,
    with our armies.
Give us Your help against our enemies,
for worthless is the assistance of humans.
Under God's leadership we shall fight
    valiantly;
He is the One Who will conquer our foes.

Psalm 60:3-7, 11-14

Prayer of Ardent Longing for God

Thirst for God

O God, You are my God for Whom I have
been searching;

for You my heart yearns and my soul thirsts
like the earth when it is parched and unable
   to give forth life without water.
For this reason I have turned my gaze toward You in the sanctuary
in order to behold Your power and Your glory,
for Your kindness is a greater gift than life;
my lips shall exalt Your glory.

Union with God

Thus will I continue to bless You while I live;
with upright hands I shall call upon Your
   Name.
As if blessed with the riches of a banquet
   my soul shall be satisfied,
and with exultant voice my mouth shall
   praise You.
I will remember You as I lie upon my bed,
and through the long hours of the night I
   will meditate on You.
You are my source of help,
and in the shadow of Your wings I shout
   joyfully.
My soul clings tightly to You;
Your right hand strengthens me.   Psalm 63:2-9

Prayer for Help against Enemies

Protection from enemies

Listen, O God, to my cry of lament;
from the fearsome enemy preserve my life.

Protect me against the crowd of those intent
  upon wicked deeds,
against the uproar of evildoers.
They sharpen their tongues like sabres,
they shoot forth their hateful words like arrows,
attacking the innocent from ambush,
suddenly shooting at them without experi-
  encing any fear.
They agree on their wicked plan;
they conspire to set traps,
saying, "Who will detect us?"
They draw up a wicked scheme
but are careful not to reveal the scheme they
  have devised;
hidden are the thoughts of each heart.

God's punishment

However, God aims His arrows at them,
and suddenly they are wounded.
Their own tongues have caused Him to take
  action against them;
all who see them nod in agreement.
As a result all will tremble at and proclaim
  the work of God,
and they will meditate on what He has done.
The just will rejoice in the Lord and seek
  refuge in Him;
all the upright will glorify Him.

Psalm 64

Prayer of Thanksgiving

Gratitude

To You we must offer our hymn of praise,
O God, in Zion.
To You our vows must be fulfilled,
You Who heed our prayers.
To You all humanity must come
because of our wicked deeds.
We are devastated by our sins;
only You can pardon them.
Blessed are those You choose
and bring to reside in Your courts.
May we be filled with the blessings of Your
house,
with the sacred objects of Your Temple.

God's bountiful harvest

You have remembered our land and wa-
tered it,
enriching it greatly.
God's reservoirs are filled;
You have prepared the grain.
Thus You have prepared the land for
growth:
drenching its furrows,
breaking up its clods,
softening it with rain showers,
blessing its yield.
You have blessed the year with Your bounty,

and Your land brings forth a rich harvest
with which the untilled meadows overflow;
rejoicing fills the hills.
The fields are covered with flocks
and the valleys are saturated with grain.
They shout and sing for joy.

Psalm 65:1-6, 10-14

Prayer for Divine Help

God, our help and deliverer

Deign, O God, to save me;
O Lord, hasten to help me. . . .
May all who search for You
exult and rejoice in Your presence.
And may those who sincerely long for Your
    salvation
say repeatedly: "May God be glorified!"
But I am afflicted and wretched;
O God, hasten to my aid!
You are my Savior and my Redeemer;
O Lord, do not delay!   Psalm 70:2, 5-6

Prayer for the Messiah's Kingdom

Just rule

O God, endow the King with the ability to
    judge rightly,
and the King's Son with a sense of justice.

He shall render fair judgment on Your people with justice
and on Your afflicted ones.
The mountains shall provide peace for the
people,
and the hills will afford justice.
He shall come to the aid of the afflicted
among His people,
rescue the children of the poor,
and overcome their oppressor.

Long and glorious reign

May He reign as long as the sun,
and, like the moon, cast His light on all generations.
He shall be like rain misting down on the
meadow,
like showers that water the earth.
Justice shall reign in His days,
and a deep-seated peace until the moon no
longer glows.

Universal dominion

May His rule extend from sea to sea,
and from the River to the farthest bounds of
the earth.
His foes shall bow down before Him,
and His enemies shall grovel in the dust.
The kings of Tarshish and the islands shall
come forward with gifts;

the kings of Arabia and Seba shall offer
 Him tribute.
All earthly kings shall pay Him homage,
all nations shall be in His service.

Defense of the poor and oppressed

For He shall come to the rescue of the poor
 when they cry out,
and of the afflicted when they have no one
 else to turn to.
He shall show pity to the lowly and the poor;
the lives of the poor He shall shelter.
From deceit and violence He shall protect
 them,
and precious to Him shall their blood be.

Prosperity of the kingdom

May He live long enough to be presented
 with the gold of Arabia
and to be prayed for without ceasing;
day by day all people shall bless Him.
May grain abound upon the earth;
on the mountain tops the crops shall spring
 forth as on Lebanon;
the city dwellers shall flourish like the vege-
 tation of the fields.
May the Lord's Name be blessed forever;
as long as the sun rises shall His name be
 exalted.

In Him all the tribes of the earth shall be
  considered blessed;
all the nations shall proclaim His greatness.

Doxology

Blessed be the Lord, the God of Israel;
no one else can work such wonders.
And may His glorious Name be blessed forever;
may the entire world be filled with His
  glory. Psalm 72

Prayer of Longing for God's Dwelling

Longing for the Sanctuary

How beautiful is Your dwelling place,
O Lord of Hosts.
My soul yearns and is filled with longing
to dwell in the courts of the Lord.
My heart and my entire being
cry out for the eternal God.
Just as the sparrow searches for a home,
and the swallow builds a nest
in which she puts her young,
so do I seek Your altars, O Lord of Hosts,
my King and my God.

Happiness of pilgrims

Happy are those who dwell in Your house,
  O Lord;

continually they offer praise to You.
Happy are those who find in You the source
    of their strength;
their hearts are eager to draw ever closer to
    You.
When they pass through tree-filled valleys
    verdant from abundant rains,
they find springs of water to quench their
    thirst.
You are the source of their strength
as they seek the God of gods in Zion.

Abode of the just

O Lord of Hosts, listen to my prayer;
do not turn away from me, O God of
    Jacob.
O God, behold our shield,
and look kindly upon the face of Your
    anointed.
I would rather experience one day in Your
    courts
than a thousand elsewhere;
I would rather lie at the outer gate of the
    house of my God
than dwell in the tents of princes who are
    wicked.
The Lord God serves as our light and our
    shield
and showers us with His grace and His glory.

The Lord is generous in bestowing every gift
upon those whose sincerity is unquestioned.
O Lord of Hosts,
those who trust in You experience true happiness.

Psalm 84

Prayer To Use Time Wisely

God's eternity and human frailty

O Lord, You have been acknowledged as
our refuge
throughout every generation.
Before the mountains were created
and the earth and the world came into existence,
You have been God throughout eternity.
By Your decree humans return to dust,
as You command: "Revert to dust, O mortals!"
For a thousand years to You
are as if they were yesterday, now that it is
past,
or as fleeting as a watch of the night.
You sanction the end of their life as they
sleep;
the following morning they resemble the
grass of the field,
which at dawn sprouts fresh and green,
but by evening has withered and faded.

Punishment for sin

Truly we are destroyed by Your wrath,
and as a result of Your anger we are beaten
  back.
You have not forgotten our iniquities;
our sins are no longer hidden from the light
  of Your scrutiny.
Our lives ebb away in the heat of Your
  wrath;
our years seem to last no longer than a sigh.
Seventy is the number of years we can an-
  ticipate,
or eighty, if we are strong.
Most of them are spent in sorrow and toil;
they pass quickly, and soon we exist no
  longer.
Who can comprehend the extent of Your
  anger
or Your indignation toward those who
  refuse to fear You?

Wisdom of heart

Teach us to realize how many days we have
  remaining
so that we may achieve true wisdom.
Be merciful, O Lord. How long will Your
  anger continue?
Take pity on Your servants!
Fill us at daybreak with Your love

so that we may joyfully sing Your praises
our entire life.
Cause us to rejoice for the days when You
afflicted us,
for the years when we were forced to contend with evil.
Let Your deeds be acknowledged by Your
servants
and Your glory by their children.
And may the graces of the Lord our God be
showered upon us
to grant success to the work of our hands.

Psalm 90

Prayer for Trust in God's Protection

God our refuge

You who abide in the shelter of the Most
High,
who dwell in the shadow of the Almighty,
say to the Lord: "You are my refuge and my
fortress,
my God, in Whom I trust."
For the Lord will rescue you from the trap
of the fowler
and save you from the virulent pestilence.
With His pinions He will shelter you,
and you shall seek shelter under His wings.
His faithfulness serves as a shield in provid-
ing protection.

You shall not have cause to fear the terror
of the night,
nor the arrow that soars through the day-
light air,
nor the pestilence that spreads extensively
in darkness,
nor the devastating plague that strikes at
midday.

Safe amid all danger

Even though a thousand may fall at your
side,
ten thousand at your right side,
such evils will not afflict you.
Rather your own eyes shall behold
the punishment inflicted on the wicked.
You have the Lord for your refuge,
since you have chosen the Most High to be
your stronghold.
No evil shall threaten you,
nor shall any affliction affect your life.

Guarded by Angels

For God has commanded His Angels
to protect you in all your activities.
With their hands they shall lift you up
lest you injure your foot against a stone.
You shall tread upon the asp and the viper;
you shall trample the lion and the dragon.

God's promise

I will deliver those who are faithful to Me;
I will set on the heights those who acknowledge My Name.
They shall cry out to Me and I will answer
  them;
I will be with them in their time of distress.
I will deliver them and cause them to be
  honored;
I will reward them with a long life
and allow them to experience My saving
  power.   Psalm 91

Prayer to the Lord Our King

An immovable throne

The Lord is King, adorned in splendor;
robed is the Lord and girt about with
  strength.
He has made the world firm,
never to be moved.
Your throne, O Lord, has stood firm from
  the beginning of time;
You have existed throughout eternity.

Mighty and Trustworthy Lord

The floods rise up, O Lord;
the seas are heard from afar;
the waves of the ocean resound.
Far more powerful than the roar of many
  waters,

more powerful than the crashing waves of
the sea—
mighty in the heavens is the Lord.
Your decrees are truly worthy of trust;
holiness has been the hallmark of Your
house,
O Lord, throughout eternity.   Psalm 93

Prayer To Worship God

Sing joyfully to the Lord

Let us sing jubilantly to the Lord,
acclaiming Him as the Rock of our salvation.
Let us greet Him with thanksgiving for everything He has done for us;
let us joyfully sing psalms of praise to Him.

He is a great God

For our Lord is a great God,
a King Who surpasses all others.
Under His power are the depths of the earth
as well as the tops of the mountains.
To Him belongs the sea, for He has created it,
and also the dry land, which His hands
have formed.

Bow down in adoration

Therefore, let us bow down to worship Him;
let us kneel in the presence of the Lord Who
made us.

For He is our God,
and we are the people He shepherds, the
flock He protects.

Heed His voice

Would that today you would listen to His
voice:
Harden not your hearts as you did at
Meribah,
as in the day of Massah in the desert,
where your fathers sought to tempt Me;
they tested Me even though they had witnessed my works.

Avoid His displeasure

For forty years I loathed that generation,
and I said: "They are a people who tend toward evil,
and they do not know My ways."
Therefore I swore in My anger:
"They shall not witness My peaceful reign."

Psalm 95

Prayer of Thanksgiving for God's Salvation

Praise His wondrous deeds

Raise your voices to the Lord with a new
song,
for He has accomplished marvelous deeds;

His right hand and His sacred arm
have won victory for Him.
The Lord has made known to all His victory;
He has given all the nations clear evidence
of His triumph.
He has never ceased in His kindness and fidelity to the house of Israel.
The farthest ends of the earth have witnessed
how our God has been triumphant.

Let all nations join in

Sing joyfully to the Lord, all you nations;
raise your voices in hymns of praise.
Let your praise of the Lord be accompanied
by the harp,
with the harp and melodious hymns.
Use trumpets and the resonance of the horn
as you sing joyfully to the King, the Lord.

Let all creation exult in Him

Let the seas and what fills them resound,
the earth and all its inhabitants.
Let the rivers roar their approval,
as the mountains accompany them with joyful shouts.
Let them do so in the presence of the Lord,
for He is coming.
His purpose is to govern the earth.

He will rule the world with propriety
and judge the nations justly.   Psalm 98

Prayer in Time of Distress

Plea for speedy aid

O Lord, listen to my prayer
as I raise my voice in supplication to You.
Do not conceal Your face from my sight
in this period of my travail.
Pay heed to my request;
do not delay in Your response, now that I
   offer my plea to You.

List of problems

For my days are fading away like smoke,
and my bones are consumed as though by
   fire.
My heart has withered and dried up like
   grass;
I neglect to nourish myself with food.
As a result of my incessant sighing
I am now nothing more than skin and
   bones.

Coming vindication by the Lord

But You, O Lord, exist for all eternity,
as will Your Name throughout all generations.
You will pay heed and show pity to Zion;

the time has come for You to bestow mercy
upon her;
the designated moment has come.
For the stones of Zion are precious to Your
servants,
and her dust causes them to weep.

Admiration of the nations

As a result the nations shall revere Your
Name, O Lord,
and all earthly kings shall sing of Your
glory,
when You have rebuilt Zion
and revealed Yourself in all Your glory,
when You have answered the prayers of
those who are destitute
and not ignored their petitions.

Psalm 102:2-6, 13-18

Prayer in Praise of God the Creator

The Lord clothed in glory

Glorify the Lord, O my soul.
O Lord, my God, You are mighty indeed.
Majesty and glory are Your garments;
light encompasses You as with a cloak.
You have spread out the heavens like a ban-
quet cloth;
You have established Your palace upon the
seas.

The clouds serve as Your chariot;
You move forth on the wings of the wind.
The winds You have appointed as Your messengers,
and flaming fire as Your ministers.
You established the earth upon a foundation
that will remain in place forever.

The Lord's creation

How countless are Your works, O Lord.
In wisdom You have created them all.
The earth abounds with Your creatures,
as is true also of Your mighty and deep oceans,
which are filled with numberless species
of living things of widely varying size,
and where ships sail forth
while the whales whom You formed frolic playfully.

Provider for all

All these look to You
to provide them with food as it is required.
When You provide it, they gather it up;
when You open Your hands, they are filled with good things.
If You conceal Your face, Your creatures are upset;
if You take away their breath, they depart this life

and return to dust.
When You send forth Your Spirit, they are
    created,
and You renew the earth.   Psalm 104:1-5, 24-30

Prayer in Honor of Christ the King

Appointed King

The Lord said to my Lord:
"Take Your seat at My right hand
and I will make Your enemies serve as Your
    footstool."
The Lord will stretch forth from Zion
the scepter that symbolizes Your power:
"Exercise Your reign in the midst of Your
    enemies.
Royal power has been Yours in holy splen-
    dor since the day of Your birth;
before the world began, like the dew, I have
    begotten You."

Anointed Priest

The Lord will not repent of the oath He has
    sworn:
"You are a priest forever,
according to the order of Melchizedek."

Victor and Judge

The Lord stands forth at Your right hand;
He will destroy kings on the day of wrath.

At the bank of a stream He will drink,
and then He will lift up His head in triumph.

Psalm 110:1-5, 7

Prayer To Be Just

Happiness of the just

Joyful are those who fear the Lord,
who rejoice greatly in obeying His commands.
Their descendants shall be powerful upon
the earth;
the honorable generation shall be blessed.
They serve as a beacon through the darkness,
as a light for the upright;
kindness, mercy, and justice are their hall-
marks.
The future bodes well for those who show
kindness to their neighbor in need,
who are just in conducting all their affairs.
They shall never be swayed from their path;
the just shall be remembered forever.

Steadfastness and generosity

They shall not be concerned about unfavor-
able news,
for their heart remains firm as they trust in
the Lord.

Since their heart is steadfast, they shall not
   be afraid
as they tower above their foes.
They bestow lavish gifts on the poor;
their generosity shall endure throughout
   eternity;
their scepter shall be exalted in glory.

Defeat of the wicked

The wicked shall behold it and be frightened;
they shall gnash their teeth and waste away;
the desires of the wicked shall never be fulfilled.   Psalm 112

Prayer of a Grateful Heart

Thanksgiving in love

I love the Lord because He has paid heed
   to me
as I begged Him to grant my prayers,
because He turned His ear to me
when I called out to Him.
The bonds of death surrounded me;
the snares of the netherworld bound me
   fast.
I was seized by distress and sorrow,
and I cried out to the Lord:
"O Lord, preserve my life!"

Petition granted

The Lord shows kindness and justice
and is merciful toward us.
The Lord watches over His little ones;
I was brought low and He rescued me.

Psalm 116:1-6

Prayer in Praise of God's Fidelity

Eternal fidelity

Glorify the Lord, all you nations.
Sing praise to Him, all you peoples.
For His kindness toward us is constant,
and the fidelity of the Lord will endure
    throughout eternity.   Psalm 117

Prayer in Praise of God's Law

Plea to do good

Teach me, O Lord, the essential details of
    Your statutes
so that I may observe them perfectly.
Grant me the gift of discernment so that I
    may observe Your Law
willingly and without hesitation.
Lead me in the path of Your commands,
for in them I take my delight.
Incline my heart to obey Your decrees,
and do not allow me to become obsessed
    with worldly profit.

Plea to avoid evil

Avert my eyes from what is vain,
for if I will follow Your way, You will grant
me life.
Fulfill for Your servant
the promise You made to those who fear
You.
Help me to avoid the reproaches that I dread,
for Your ordinances are salutary.
Behold, I long for Your Commandments;
in Your justice grant me life.

Meditation on the Law

I truly love Your Law, O Lord.
On it I meditate throughout the day.
Your command has given me wisdom far
surpassing that of my enemies,
for it is always in my heart.
My knowledge surpasses that of all my
teachers
when I meditate on Your decrees.
My powers of discernment are superior to
those of the elders
because I heed Your precepts.

Wisdom leads to goodness

I refuse to stray on evil paths
lest I fail to observe Your precepts.
I refuse to ignore Your ordinances,

for You have taught me.
Your promises are sweet-tasting to my palate,
even sweeter than honey to my taste.
I have achieved greater wisdom from Your
    precepts;
therefore all evil deeds are abhorrent to me.

God's Word—light of life

Your Word serves as a lamp to my feet,
affording light to my path.
With a solemn promise I have sworn
to obey Your laws, all of which are just.
I have been greatly afflicted.
O Lord, come to my aid as You have prom-
    ised.
Receive, O Lord, the homage I offer You
and instruct me about Your decrees.

God's Law—joy of the heart

Though my life is in constant danger,
I do not neglect obedience to Your Law.
Even though the wicked seek to entrap me,
I have not ceased to heed Your precepts.
Your decrees are my eternal inheritance;
they are the source of joy to my heart.
My heartfelt determination is to obey Your
    laws
at all times and in every respect.

Psalm 119:33-40, 97-112

Prayer to the Lord Our Protector

Trust in God

I lift up my gaze toward the mountains;
from what source can I look for help?
My only true help will come from the Lord,
the Creator of heaven and earth.

Ever-vigilant Lord

God will not permit your feet to stray;
as your guardian He will not allow His at-
tention to wander.
In that role He will neither slumber nor
sleep,
the Guardian of Israel.

Deliverance from evil

The Lord serves as your Guardian;
the Lord is your protective shade;
He stations Himself beside you at your right
hand.
You shall not be harmed by the sun during
the day,
nor by the moon at night.
The Lord will guard you from every form of
evil;
He will continuously guard your life.
The Lord will oversee your coming and
your going,
both now and throughout your life.   Psalm 121

Prayer in Spiritual Need

Look to our heavenly helper

To You, O Lord, I lift up my gaze,
to You Whose throne is in heaven.
As the eyes of a servant
focus on the hands of his master,
as the eyes of a maid
focus on the hands of her mistress,
so do our eyes focus on the Lord our God
in the confident hope that He will show us
   mercy.

Prayer for God's mercy

Have pity on us, O Lord, and grant us Your
   mercy,
for we have endured far more than our
   share of contempt.
We have been afflicted
as the insolent mock and taunt us
and the arrogant treat us with contempt.

Psalm 123

Prayer for Spiritual Renewal

Redeemed by the Lord

When the Lord showered His blessings on
   Zion,
at first we thought we were dreaming.
But then we were overcome with laughter,

and our mouths uttered songs of joy.
Then the nations were forced to admit:
"The Lord has done great things for them."
Truly the Lord has done great things for us,
and we were filled with joy.
Restore our times of prosperity, O Lord,
as You did when You caused heavy rains to fill
    arid river beds.

Everlasting reward

Those who sow in tears
shall reap with shouts of joy.
Although they go forth with copious weep-
    ing
as they carry the seed to be sown,
they shall rejoice on their return
as they carry their sheaves.   Psalm 126

Prayer for a Good Home Life

Blessings of a good family

Blessed are you who fear the Lord,
who follow in His path.
For you shall enjoy the fruits of your labor;
you shall be blessed with happiness and
    prosperity.
Your wife shall be like a fertile vine
that blossoms in your home;
your children shall be like olive plants
as they gather around your table.

In the same way will the person be blessed
who fears the Lord.

Prosperity and long life

May the Lord shower you with blessings
  from Zion
every day of your life.
May you share in the prosperity of Jerusalem
and live to see your children's children.
May peace be granted to Israel.   <small>Psalm 128</small>

Prayer for Pardon and Peace

Plea to be heard

From the depths of my misery I call out to
  You, O Lord.
Lord, listen to my plea.
Allow Your ears to be attentive
as I raise my voice in petition to You.

God's pardon

If You, O Lord, record our sins,
who can stand before You unashamed?
But You grant us forgiveness
and deserve to be revered.

Trust in God's mercy

My trust is in the Lord;
my soul has faith in His Word.

My soul awaits the arrival of the Lord
more than sentries await the coming of dawn.

Hope in the Redemption

More than sentries await the dawn,
let Israel wait for the Lord.
For with the Lord one can expect kindness
and hope to experience the fullness of redemption.
And He will forgive the people of Israel
for all their wicked deeds.   Psalm 130

Prayer of Humble Trust in God

Self-abasement before God

O Lord, I am not proud of heart
and my eyes are not haughty.
I do not concern myself with matters of
   worldly importance
nor with things that are beyond the scope of
   my intelligence.
Rather, I have quieted my soul,
calming it as though it were a weaned child.
Like a weaned child sitting on its mother's
   lap,
so is my soul within me.

Call to hope in the Lord

O Israel, continue to trust in the Lord,
both now and forever.   Psalm 131

Prayer for Fraternal Charity

Holy unity

Behold, how delightful it is, and how in-
    spiring,
when kindred dwell in unity.
It is comparable to when the precious oint-
    ment upon the head
runs down over the beard, the beard of
    Aaron,
and down the collar of his robe.
It is a dew similar to that of Hermon
descending upon the mountains of Zion;
for there the Lord has bestowed His greatest
    blessing, life everlasting.   Psalm 133

Prayer in Praise of God,
the Benefactor of His People

Exhortation to God's servants

Praise the Name of the Lord;
offer praise, you servants of the Lord
who congregate in the house of the Lord,
in the courtyards of the house of our God.
Give praise to the Lord, for He is good;
sing praise to His Name, which is beloved
    by us.
For the Lord has designated Jacob as His
    own,
Israel as His special possession.

God's greatness

I fully realize that the Lord is great;
our Lord surpasses all other gods.
Everything that the Lord wills He accomplishes
in heaven and on earth,
in the oceans and in all the watery depths.
He raises storm clouds to appear from the ends of the earth;
He makes the rain and lightning
and calls forth the winds from His storehouse.

Protector of His people

Your Name, O Lord, will endure forever,
as will Your renown through all generations.
For the Lord rises in defense of His people
and bestows mercy on His servants.
The idols of the pagan nations are composed of silver and gold
and are fashioned by human hands.
They have mouths but they cannot speak;
they have eyes but they cannot see.
They have ears but they cannot hear;
no breath pours forth from their mouths.
Those who made them shall be like them,
as will everyone who trusts in them.

Psalm 135:1-7, 13-18

Prayer in Thanksgiving for
God's Kindness

Give thanks

Give thanks to the Lord, for He is good,
for His mercy endures forever.
Give thanks to the God of gods,
for His mercy endures forever.
Give thanks to the Lord of lords,
for His mercy endures forever.

For creation

He alone has wrought great wonders;
His mercy endures forever.
He made the heavens according to His wisdom;
His mercy endures forever.
He spread out the earth upon the waters;
His mercy endures forever.
He made the great heavenly lights;
His mercy endures forever.
He devised the sun to rule over the day;
His mercy endures forever.
He created the moon and the stars to rule
over the night;
His mercy endures forever.

For salvation

He did not forget us in our misery;
His mercy endures forever.

He freed us from the grasp of our enemies;
His mercy endures forever.
He supplies food for all living things;
His mercy endures forever.
Give thanks to the God of heaven,
for His mercy endures forever.

Psalm 136:1-9, 23-26

Prayer to the All-Knowing and Ever-Present God

The all-knowing God

O Lord, You have studied me and You
    know me completely.
You know when I sit and when I stand;
You comprehend my thoughts from afar.
You are aware of my travels and my rest;
with all my activities You are familiar.
Even before a word passes my lips, O Lord,
You know exactly what I intend to say.
From behind me and in front of me You
    surround me
and rest Your hand upon me.
Such knowledge is far beyond my under-
    standing,
too lofty for me to comprehend.

The all-present God

How can I hide from Your spirit?
How can I flee from Your presence?

If I ascend to the heavens, You await me;
if I descend to the netherworld, You are
  there too.
If I travel to the easternmost part of the
  world
or if I settle at the farthest limits of the west,
even then Your hand shall be there to guide
  me
and Your right hand to hold me fast.
If I say, "Surely the dark shall conceal me,
and the night shall be to me like the day,"
I forget that for You darkness itself is not
  dark
and the night shines as brightly as the day.
Darkness and light are identical in Your
  eyes.

The all-provident Creator

I know that You have designed my innermost being;
You formed me in my mother's womb.
I give You thanks that You have made me
  so wonderfully;
awe-inspiring are Your works.
When I was being formed in secret,
when I was fashioned in the womb,
You knew everything about me;
even my physical makeup was not un-
  known to You.

Prior to my conception You foreknew every
    detail of my life;
in Your book my actions were all recorded;
the number of my days was preordained
    even before one of them ever existed.

The compassionate and saving God

How meaningful to me are Your designs, O
    God;
how incredibly vast is their scope.
If I were to count them, they would out-
    number the sands of the sea;
to complete that task I would need more
    than the days of life allotted to me.
Examine me, O God, so that my heart con-
    ceals no secret from You;
test me so that You may know my thoughts.
If I should turn aside from Your paths,
lead me back to my former ways.

Psalm 139:1-18, 23-24

Prayer in Time of Abandonment

Cry of one trapped in misery

With a vibrant voice I cry out to the Lord;
with a strong voice I beg the Lord for help.
I pour out my complaint in His presence;
before Him I reveal my deep distress.
O Lord, when my spirit grows faint within
    me,

You know the path I should travel.
On the ways along which I walk
my enemies have set a trap for me.
I look around on all sides,
but no one is willing to come to my aid.
I have no means of escape;
there is no one who is concerned for my life.

Call to the Lord for help

I cry out to You, O Lord,
for You are my refuge,
my only source of hope in the land of the
    living.
Answer my cry for help,
for I have been brought low indeed.
Rescue me, O Lord, from my persecutors,
who are too powerful for me to overcome.
Lead me in safety from my difficult situa-
    tion
so that I may give thanks to Your Name.
The just shall be willing to listen to me
when they see how good You have been to
    me.   Psalm 142

Prayer of a Penitent in Distress

Call upon God's fidelity

O Lord, listen to my prayer;
hearken to my plea as a sign of Your faith-
    fulness;

show Your justice and answer me.
And do not seek to render judgment on
Your servant,
since before You no one living can be regarded as just.

Encircled by evil

For my enemy pursues me;
he has crushed my life to the ground.
He has left me lying in the darkness
like those who have long been dead.
Therefore my spirit grows faint within me;
my heart within me is overwhelmed with
dread.

Plea to be heard

I recall the days of old;
I meditate on all Your deeds;
the works of Your hands I remember.
I stretch out my hands as I implore Your
help;
as parched land thirsts for water,
so does my soul thirst for You.
Hasten to answer my prayer, O Lord,
for I have become despondent in spirit.
Do not hide Your face from me,
for I do not wish to become like those who
descend into the pit.

Request to walk justly

At dawn let me hear of Your kindness
for in You I place my trust.
Show me the path along which I should walk,
for to You I lift up my soul.
Rescue me from my enemies, O Lord,
for in You I place my hope.
Teach me to do Your will,
for You are my God.
May Your Spirit guide me
to keep to a straight path.
For the sake of Your Name, O Lord, save
    my life;
in Your justice free me from distress.

Psalm 143:1-11

Prayer in Praise of God's Goodness

Praise of God's greatness

I will offer praise to You, my God and my
    King,
and I will glorify Your Name forever and
    ever.
Every day I will exalt You,
and I will bless Your Name forever and ever.
Mighty is the Lord and deserving of the
    highest praise;
His grandeur is beyond measure.
Every generation extols Your works
and proclaims Your power.

They speak of the glory of Your illustrious majesty
and recount Your awesome works.
They recount the power of Your mighty deeds
and portray Your greatness.

God's mercy

They narrate the tales of Your abundant mercy
and joyfully sing of the justice You have shown.
The Lord is sympathetic and tender-hearted,
not prone to anger and always ready to prove His great kindness.
The Lord is generous to all
and shows compassion to everything He has created.

God's power

Let all Your creation give You thanks, O Lord,
and let Your faithful servants bless You.
Let them relate the glory of Your Kingdom
and speak of Your power,
making known to humans Your mighty deeds
and the magnificent splendor of Your Kingdom.
Your Kingdom shall endure for all ages,

and Your dominion shall never cease through all generations.

God's providence

The Lord is trustworthy in all His words,
and He is holy in all His works.
The Lord raises up all who are falling
and elevates all who have been bowed down.
The eyes of all look to You with hope,
and You provide them with the necessary sustenance.
By merely opening Your hands
You satisfy the needs of every living creature.

God's justice

The Lord shows justice in all His actions
and is holy in all His deeds.
The Lord is never far away from those who call upon Him,
from those who call upon Him in their need.
The Lord answers the prayers of those who fear Him;
He hears their pleas and rescues them.
The Lord keeps close to His heart all those who love Him,
but those who are wicked He will destroy.

Praise from all

My lips will recount Your praiseworthy deeds, O Lord.

May all Your creatures bless Your holy
Name forever and ever.   Psalm 145

Prayer of Trust in God Alone

Living praise

Offer praise to the Lord, my soul;
I shall praise the Lord throughout my entire
    life;
I shall sing hymns of praise to my God
    while I live.

Human frailty

Do not place your trust in princes,
for they are merely mortal beings who are
    powerless to ensure your salvation.
When their spirit departs from their body,
    they return to dust;
on that day all their plans will serve no pur-
    pose for the future.

God's power and fidelity

Blessed are those whose source of help is the
    God of Jacob,
who place their hope in the Lord their God,
the Creator of heaven and earth,
the seas and all that exists.
The Lord is forever faithful to His Word,
ensures justice for those who are oppressed,
and provides food for the hungry.

God's saving works

The Lord frees prisoners;
the Lord grants sight to the blind.
The Lord raises up the lowly;
the Lord loves the just.
The Lord offers protection to the stranger;
the orphan and the widow He supports,
but the way of the wicked He thwarts.

Eternal Kingdom

The Lord shall reign forever.
He shall be your God, O Zion, through all
    generations.   Psalm 146

Prayer to God Who Sustains Us

Praise befits the Lord

Offer praise to God for His goodness;
sing praise to our God for the graces He be-
    stows upon us;
how fitting it is to praise Him.
The Lord rebuilds Jerusalem,
gathering there the dispersed of Israel.
He offers solace to the brokenhearted
and bandages their wounds.

Mighty and merciful God

The Lord knows the total number of the
    stars,
and He has given a name to each one.

The Lord is great, and limitless is His power;
the depth of His wisdom cannot be measured.
The Lord raises up the lowly,
but the wicked He casts to the ground.

Diligent Sustainer

Sing songs of thanksgiving to the Lord,
sing to our God hymns of praise accompa-
    nied by the harp.
For He fills the heavens with clouds,
provides rain for the earth,
and causes grass to sprout on the moun-
    tains.
He supplies food to the cattle
and to the ravens when they cry out to Him.

Delights in His faithful ones

The strength of a steed causes the Lord no
    delight,
nor does He take pleasure in the swiftness
    of a runner.
The Lord delights in those who fear Him,
in those who hope to be the beneficiaries of
    His kindness.

Deliverance for His people

Glorify the Lord, O Jerusalem;
offer praise to your God, O Zion.
For He has fortified your gates,
and He has blessed your children who dwell
    in your territory.

The Lord has granted peace within your
   borders;
with the finest wheat He fills your stomachs.
He sends forth His commands to His people
   on earth;
His Word reaches us swiftly.

Keeper of His Word

He spreads snow as though it were wool;
frost He scatters like ashes.
He disperses hail like crumbs;
the waters freeze from the intensity of His
   cold.
Then He sends forth His Word and causes
   them to melt;
when the breezes blow, the waters begin to
   flow.
The Lord has proclaimed His Word to Jacob;
He has revealed His statutes and His ordinances to Israel.
He has not granted this privilege to any
   other nation;
He has not revealed His laws to them.

Psalm 147

Prayer in Praise of God

Praise from the heavens

Offer praise to the Lord from the heavens,
praise Him from the heights.

Offer praise to Him, all you His Angels,
praise Him, all you His hosts.
Offer praise to Him, sun and moon,
praise Him, all you shining stars.
Offer praise to Him, you highest heavens,
and you waters above the heavens.
Let them all praise the Name of the Lord,
for when He issued His command, they
    were created;
He created them for an eternal existence,
assigning them laws that can never be abro-
    gated.

Praise from the earth

Praise the Lord from the earth,
you sea monsters and all the depths of the
    sea,
you lightning and hail, snow and clouds,
you storm winds that fulfill His Word;
you mountains and all you hills,
you fruit trees and all you cedars;
you wild beasts and all you tame animals,
you creatures that crawl and fly.
Earthly kings and all peoples,
princes and judges of the earth,
young men and maidens,
old men and boys—
let them all praise the Name of the Lord,
for His Name alone is exalted.

The majesty of the Lord is exalted above
  earth and heaven;
He has magnified the strength of His people.
Let Him be praised by all His faithful ones,
the children of Israel, the people close to Him.
Alleluia.   Psalm 148

Prayer of Praise Offered by All Creation

Let all creation praise God

Praise the Lord in His heavenly domain;
praise Him in the stronghold of His firmament.
Praise Him for His mighty deeds;
praise Him for His majestic sovereignty.

Praise God in every way

Praise Him with trumpet blasts,
praise Him with lyre and harp,
praise Him with tambourines and dancing,
praise Him with flutes and stringed instruments.
Praise Him with crashing cymbals,
praise Him with clanging cymbals.
Let everything that has the breath of life
offer praise to the Lord.
Alleluia.   Psalm 150

JESUS — MAN OF ASSIDUOUS PRAYER

As a faithful Jew, Jesus undoubtedly recited those prayers that were commonly said by devout Jews of His day. Among these were the **Shema** ("Hear, O Israel") recited as a creed each morning and night, and the **Tefillah** (eighteen benedictions) recited at sunrise, mid-afternoon, and sunset. He was also accustomed to taking part in the sabbath day synagogue services (Luke 4:16).

THE PRAYERS OF JESUS

JESUS lived His entire life in communion with God, so that the attitude of prayer was for Him a permanent one. Reference is made in the Gospels on several occasions to His withdrawal to desert places for refreshment and solace of spirit (see Matthew 14:13; Mark 6:32; Luke 4:42).

In addition, Jesus prayed at important occasions of His public ministry: before His Baptism (Luke 3:21), before the call of His disciples (Luke 6:12-13), on the occasion of many of His miracles (Luke 9:16; see John 6:23; Mark 7:34; 9:29; John 9:30-33; 11:41f), before the Eucharistic promise (Matthew 14:23), before the promise of the primacy to Peter (Luke 9:18), at His Transfiguration (Luke 9:28) and both before and during His Passion (Luke 22:39-46; Matthew 27:46; Luke 22:32; 23:34; 23:46; John 17).

Jesus prayed for the glorification of His Father (John 2:27-28), and for His own glorification (John 17:1-5); He prayed for His Apostles (John 17:6-19), and in particular for Peter (Luke 22:31-32); He prayed for all the faithful (John 17:20-26) and for His enemies (Luke 23:34). He also taught His disciples the Our Father (Matthew 6:9-13).

Thus, His whole life was one of prayer inasmuch as He was constantly offering acts of worship, praise, and thanksgiving to His heavenly Father. Now seated at the right hand of God the Father, Jesus continues to pray for us. He intercedes for us (Romans 8:34), appears before God on our behalf (Hebrews 9:24), and is our Advocate with the Father (1 John 2:1). His prayers can be an inspiration to our prayer life, for we also have been given a task to do on this earth and have been sent by the Father to carry on the work of Jesus.

PRAYERS DURING THE PUBLIC MINISTRY

The Lord's Prayer

Our Father,
Who art in heaven,
hallowed be Thy Name.
Thy Kingdom come.
Thy will be done
on earth as it is in heaven.
Give us this day our daily bread,
and forgive us our trespasses
as we forgive those who trespass against us.
And lead us not into temptation,
but deliver us from evil.

Matthew 6:9-13

Jesus' Praise of the Father

Father,
Lord of heaven and earth,
I offer praise to You,
for what You have hidden from the edu-
    cated and the clever
You have made known to children.
Father, all this is true,
in accordance with Your wise design.

Matthew 11:25-26

Jesus' Prayer at the Tomb of Lazarus

Father,
I thank You for having listened to Me.
I know that You always listen to Me,
but I have said this for the benefit of the
    people
so that they may come to believe that You
    sent Me.   John 11:41-42

Jesus' Prayer for His Father's Glorification

Father,
My soul is now in a state of distress,
yet what should I say?
Father, save Me from having to endure this
    hour?
But it was for this reason that I came to this
    hour.
Father, may Your Name be glorified.
         John 12:27-28

PRAYERS DURING THE PASSION

Jesus' Prayer for His Own Glorification

Father,
the moment has finally arrived.
Give glory to Your Son

so that Your Son may give glory to You in
   turn,
for You have given Him authority over all
   humankind
in order that He may bestow the gift of eternal life
on those You gave to Him.

Eternal life is this:
the knowledge of You, the only true God,
and Him Whom You sent, Jesus Christ.

I glorified You on earth
by accomplishing what You wanted Me to
   do.
Therefore, Father, now allow Me once again
   to share Your glory,
the glory that I had with You before the creation of the world.   John 17:1-5

Jesus' Prayer in the Garden

My Father,
if it is at all possible,
let Me avoid this cup of suffering.
Yet let everything be in accordance with
   Your will
and not as I wish.

My Father,
if it is not possible for this cup to pass Me by
without My first drinking of it,
then let Your will be done.

Matthew 26:39, 42

Jesus' Prayer for His Disciples

Father, I have made Your Name known
to those You placed under My care in the
world.
They belonged to You and You entrusted
them to Me;
they have remained faithful to Your Word.
They are fully aware
that everything You gave Me has You as its
source.
The message You entrusted to Me
I in turn entrusted to them,
and they acknowledged its truth.
They truly realize that I came from You,
and they believe that You were the One
Who sent Me.

For these I pray—
not for the world but for the ones You have
given Me,
for they truly belong to You.
Everything that belongs to Me is Yours,
and everything that belongs to You is Mine;
in them I have been glorified.

I will no longer be in the world,
but these will remain in the world
as I come to You.

Most holy Father,
protect them with Your Name that You
    have given Me
so that they may be one, just as We are one.
As long as I was in their company,
I afforded them the protection of Your
    Name that You gave Me.
I watched over them diligently
and not a single one of them was lost,
aside from the one who was destined to be
    lost
in fulfillment of Scripture;
now allow Me to come to You.
I say all these things while I am still in the
    world
so that they may share in My joy com-
    pletely.

I gave them Your Word,
and the world has hated them,
because they do not belong to the world
any more than I belong to the world.
I do not ask You to remove them from the
    world,
but that You protect them from the evil one.
They do not belong to the world

any more than I belong to the world.
Sanctify them by means of truth.
Your Word is truth.

Just as You sent Me into the world,
so I have sent them into the world.
I sanctify Myself now for them
so that they may be sanctified in truth.

John 17:6-19

Jesus' Prayer for All Believers

Father, I do not pray simply for those
   whom You entrusted to Me;
I also pray for those who will believe in Me
   through their testimony,
so that all may be one,
as You, Father, are in Me and I am in
   You.
May they be one in Us
in order that the world may come to believe
   that You sent Me.
I have given them the glory You gave Me
so that they may be one as We are one—
I living in them, You living in Me—
and thus their unity may be complete.
In this way the world will know that You
   sent Me
and that You loved them just as You loved
   Me.

Father,
all those You entrusted to My care
I wish to be in My company in heaven
and to behold My glory,
which You bestowed on Me
because of the love You had for Me before
the creation of the world.

Just Father,
those You entrusted to Me do not know You,
but I know You,
and they are aware that You sent Me.
To them I have made known Your Name,
and I will continue to do so,
in order that the love You have for Me may
live in them,
and I too may live in them.   John 17:20-26

Jesus' Prayer on the Cross

My God,
My God,
why have You
forsaken Me?   Matthew 27:46

Jesus' Prayer for His Enemies

My Father,
forgive them,

for they do not realize
what they are doing.   Luke 23:34

Jesus' Final Prayer

Father,
into Your hands
I commend
My Spirit.   Luke 23:46

THE EARLY CHURCH — UNITED IN PRAYER

The early Christians devoted themselves to the apostolic instruction and the communal life, to the breaking of bread and the prayers. With exultant and sincere hearts they took their meals in common, praising God and winning the approval of all the people.

PRAYERS OF THE EARLY CHURCH

FROM the beginning the first Christians were conscious of being a people of prayer. This flowed from their Israelite origin as well as from the instructions and example of Jesus. While waiting for the coming of the Holy Spirit, Who had been promised by Jesus, the Apostles gathered in prayer with Mary and the other relatives of Jesus (Acts 1:14).

After the Spirit's coming and under His inspiration, the early Christians took part in communal prayer, including the Eucharist, and in Temple worship (Acts 2:42-47). They prayed for boldness in proclaiming God's Word (Acts 4:24-31) and elected ministers to leave the Apostles free to do their primary work of prayer and preaching (Acts 6:4).

At first the Christians were led to sing and then to imitate the Psalms of the Old Testament. Soon, however, they began to compose prayers of their own—in keeping with the idea of their union with one another in Christ. This gave rise to the use of canticles and thanksgiving prayers in liturgical celebrations as well as in private prayers.

Some of the most famous examples of these are the so-called Gospel canticles—the Magnificat *of Mary, the* Benedictus *of Zechariah, and the* Nunc Dimittis *of Simeon (Luke 1—2) as well as the canticles and thanksgivings found throughout Paul's Epistles (Ephesians 5:14; 1 Timothy 3:6; 2 Timothy 2:11) and the Book of Revelation (4:11; 5:12).*

Christians are invited to make these prayers their own, so as to recover that fervent faith and single-minded outlook which were characteristic of the early days of the Church.

PRAYERS FROM THE GOSPELS AND ACTS

Canticle of Mary

The soul rejoices in the Lord

I will proclaim the grandeur of the Lord;
my spirit finds its joy in God my Savior.
For He has looked upon His handmaid in
   her lowliness;
all future generations shall call me blessed.
God Who is all-powerful has done wondrous deeds for me,
and blessed is His Name.
His mercy has been shown throughout every
   age
to those who fear Him.

The Lord has shown great power with His
   arm;
He has bewildered the proud in their inmost
   thoughts.
He has unseated the mighty from their
   thrones
and raised up the lowly.
The hungry He has provided with every
   choice food
while the rich He has sent away unfed.
He has given unfailing support to Israel His
   servant,

always mindful of His mercy,
as He promised our fathers,
promised Abraham and His descendants
   forever.   Luke 1:46-55

Canticle of Zechariah

The Messiah and His forerunner

Blessed be the Lord, the God of Israel,
because He has come to dwell among His
   people and redeem them.
He has raised a horn of salvation for us
in the house of David His servant,
as He had promised through the mouths of
   His holy Prophets
from ancient times:
that we would be saved from our enemies
and rescued from the hands of all our foes.
The Lord has shown unceasing mercy to
   our ancestors
and never forgotten His Covenant,
or the oath He swore to Abraham our father
that, freed from fear and delivered from our
   enemies,
we would serve Him with true devotion
and be holy in His sight for all our days.

And you, O child, shall be called
the Prophet of the Most High.

For you shall go before the Lord
to prepare the people to receive Him,
giving His people the knowledge that salva-
    tion is theirs
once their sins have been forgiven.
All this is the result of the kindness of our
    God;
as our Dawn, He shall visit us in His mercy
to shine on those who sit in darkness
and in the shadow of death,
to guide our feet along the path of peace.

Luke 1:68-79

Canticle of Simeon

*Christ is the light of the nations
and the glory of Israel*

Now, Master, You can allow Your servant
    to depart in peace,
for You have fulfilled Your Word.
My eyes have witnessed Your salvation
displayed for all the peoples to see:
a light of revelation for the Gentiles
and the glory of Your people Israel.

Luke 2:29-32

Prayer for Signs and Wonders

Sovereign Lord,
Creator of heaven and earth and the sea

and all that is in them,
inspired by the Holy Spirit You have said
through the words of our father David Your
  servant:
"Why did the Gentiles become enraged
and the peoples engage in acts of folly?
The kings of the earth were united,
the princes had joined together
against the Lord and against His anointed."

In fact they gathered in this very city
against Your holy Servant Jesus, Whom
  You anointed:
Herod and Pontius Pilate who were aligned
  with the Gentiles,
and the people of Israel.
Everything they did resulted in the very
  things
that in Your prudence and Your power
You had designed in ages past.

But now, O Lord, You must be aware of the
  threats
they are leveling against us.
Give Your servants the power
to reveal Your Word confidently.
Stretch forth Your hand
so that healings, signs, and wonders
may be effected in the Name of Jesus, Your
  holy Servant.   Acts 4:24-30

PRAYERS FROM THE PAULINE EPISTLES

Prayer in Praise of God's Wisdom and Knowledge

How deep are the riches and the wisdom
and the knowledge of God!
How incomprehensible are His judgments,
how unsearchable are His ways!
For who has known the mind of the Lord
or served as His advisor?
Or who has given Him anything
and thereby been deserving of a reward?
From Him,
and through Him,
and for Him,
all things exist.
To Him be glory forever.   Romans 11:33-36

Prayer in Praise of Divine Love

If in speaking I use human tongues
and angelic as well,
but do not have love,
I am nothing more than an ear-splitting
    gong, a banging cymbal.
If I have the gift of prophecy
and am blessed with complete knowledge
so that I can fully understand every mys-
    tery,

if my faith is so great that I am able to move
  mountains,
but do not have love,
I am nothing.

If I give away all my earthly possessions
and hand over my body as well,
but do not have love,
I achieve nothing.

Love is tolerant,
love is charitable.
Love is not envious,
it does not have an inflated opinion of itself,
it is not filled with its own importance.
Love is never obnoxious,
it does not seek its own advantage.
It is not prone to anger,
nor does it brood over setbacks.
Love does not rejoice about what is evil
but rejoices in the truth.
Love bears all things,
believes and hopes all things,
endures all things.

Love never fails;
prophecies will eventually cease,
tongues will become silent,
knowledge will pass away.
Our knowledge is partial
and our prophesying is partial,

but when we encounter the perfect,
what is imperfect will pass away.
When I was a child,
I used to talk like a child,
think like a child,
reason like a child.
However, when I became a man
I put all childish ways aside.

At the moment we see indistinctly, as in a
    mirror;
then we shall see face to face.
My knowledge is only partial now;
then I shall know fully even as I am known.
There are three things that endure:
faith, hope, and love,
and the greatest of these is love.

1 Corinthians 13:1-13

Prayer of Thanksgiving after Affliction

Praised be God,
the Father of our Lord Jesus Christ,
the Father of all mercy
Who is the source of our consolation.
God offers us comfort when we are afflicted,
and thus He enables us to comfort those who
    are troubled,
as we offer the same consolation we have re-
    ceived from Him.   2 Corinthians 1:3-4

Prayer to God Who Saves Us

Praised be the God and Father
of our Lord Jesus Christ
Who in His gift of Christ has bestowed on
us
every spiritual blessing that exists in
heaven.

God chose us in Christ
before the creation of the world
to be holy
and blameless in His sight.

He predestined us
to be His adopted children through Jesus
Christ—
such was the design that pleased Him—
so that all might offer Him praise for the
glorious favor
He has bestowed on us in His beloved.

In Him and through His Blood
we have been redeemed
and our sins have been forgiven,
so immeasurably generous
is God's kindness to us.

God has granted us the wisdom
to understand completely the mystery,
the plan it pleased Him
to decree in Christ.

This plan was to be carried out in Christ,
in the fullness of time,
so that all things might be brought into
    unity in Him
in the heavens and on the earth.   Ephesians 1:3-10

Prayer for the Church

I kneel before God the Father,
from Whom every family in heaven and on
    earth takes its name,
and I pray that He will bestow gifts on you
in accordance with the riches of His glory.
May He strengthen you inwardly
through the working of His Spirit.
May Christ dwell in your hearts through faith,
so that charity will be the root and founda-
    tion of your life.

In this way you will be able to fully grasp,
with all the holy ones,
the breadth and length and height and depth
of the love of Christ
and experience this love that surpasses all
    knowledge,
so that you may attain the complete pres-
    ence of God Himself.

God, Whose power is now at work in us,
is able to accomplish immeasurably more
    than we can ask or imagine.

To Him be glory in the Church and in
Christ Jesus
through all generations, forever and ever.

Ephesians 3:14-21

Prayer for Peace, Love, and Faith

May God the Father and our Lord Jesus
Christ
grant peace and love and faith to the whole
community.
May every grace be bestowed on all
who love our Lord Jesus Christ
without reservation.   Ephesians 6:23-24

Prayer of Praise to Christ the Lord

Though He possessed the form of God,
Jesus did not deem equality with God
as something to be avidly sought.

Rather, He emptied Himself
and adopted the form of a slave,
being born in the likeness of men.

Recognized as being of human estate,
He humbled Himself,
obediently accepting even death,
death on a Cross.

As a result, at Jesus' Name
every knee should bend

in the heavens, on the earth,
and under the earth,
and every tongue proclaim
to the glory of God the Father
that Jesus Christ is Lord.   Philippians 2:6-11

Prayer of Thanksgiving to the Father for Choosing Us

Let us give thanks to God the Father
Who has made you worthy
to share in the inheritance of the Saints
in light.

He saved us from the power of darkness
and brought us into the Kingdom
of His beloved Son.
Through Him we now have redemption
and the forgiveness of our sins.

Jesus is the image of the invisible God,
the first-born of all creatures.
In Him everything in heaven and on earth
    was created,
both visible and invisible.

All were created through Him;
all were created for Him.
He existed prior to every other thing,
and without Him nothing could continue to
    exist.

He is the Head of the Body, the Church;
He is the Beginning,
the First-born of the dead,
and primacy is His in everything.

It was God's Will to make absolute fullness
reside in His Son
and, by means of Him, to reconcile everything,
both on earth and in the heavens,
making peace through the Blood of His
Cross.   Colossians 1:12-20

Prayer of Praise for the Glory of Jesus

Wonderful indeed is the mystery of our
Faith
that we are overjoyed to profess.
Christ was manifested in the flesh,
vindicated in the Spirit,
seen by the Angels,
preached among the Gentiles,
believed in throughout the world,
taken up in glory.   1 Timothy 3:16

Prayer in Praise of God as the King of Kings

God is our blessed and sole Ruler,
the King of kings and the Lord of lords.
He alone is immortal

and dwells in unapproachable light.
No human being has ever seen Him
or can see Him.

To Him be honor
and everlasting power.   1 Timothy 6:15-16

PRAYERS FROM THE
CATHOLIC EPISTLES

Prayer of Praise to God for Giving Us
New Birth

Praised be the God and Father
of our Lord Jesus Christ.
He gave us a new birth—
a birth unto hope whose source of life
is the Resurrection of Jesus Christ from the
    dead;
a birth to an imperishable inheritance
that cannot fade or be defiled
and that is kept in heaven for you
who with God's power are protected
    through faith;
a birth to a salvation that will be revealed
at the end of time.

1 Peter 1:3-5

Prayer in Praise of Christ
· Who Suffered for Us

Jesus Christ suffered for us,
leaving us an example
to follow in His footsteps.

He perpetrated no evil deed;
no deceitful word ever issued from His
mouth.
When He was insulted,
He did not respond with an insult.

When He was subjected to suffering,
He did not issue threats.
Instead He delivered Himself up
to the One Who judges with justice.

In His own Body
He carried our sins to the Cross,
so that all of us, free from sin,
could live in accordance with God's will.

By the wounds of Christ you were healed.
1 Peter 2:21-24

Prayer in Praise of God Our Savior

There is One Who can prevent you from
falling
and allow you to stand unstained and exultant
in the presence of His glory.

To the only God our Savior,
through Jesus Christ our Lord,
be glory and majesty,
power and authority,
before all ages,
now and for all ages to come.   Jude 24-25

PRAYERS FROM THE BOOK OF REVELATION

Prayer of Praise to Jesus Our Redeemer

O Lord our God,
You are worthy of glory, honor, and power,
for You have made all things;
by a mere act of Your will they came into
    existence and were created.

You are worthy, O Lord,
to receive the scroll and break open its seals.
For You were crucified,
and with Your Blood You purchased for
    God
persons of every race and tongue,
of every people and nation.

You made them a Kingdom
of priests to serve our God,
and they shall reign on the earth.

Worthy is the Lamb Who was slain
to receive power and riches,
wisdom and strength,
honor and glory and praise.

Revelation 4:11; 5:9-10, 12

Prayer in Praise of God Our Judge

We offer praise to You, Lord God Almighty,
You Who are and Who always were.
You have assumed Your mighty power,
and established Your reign.

The nations raged in their anger,
but then came Your day of wrath
and the moment for the dead to be judged,
the time to reward Your servants the
    Prophets
and the holy ones who fear Your Name,
the great and the small alike.

Now have salvation and power come,
the reign of our God
and the authority of His Anointed One.
For the accuser of our brothers and sisters
    has been cast out,
the devil who day and night accused them
    before God.

They conquered him by the Blood of the
    Lamb
and by the truth of their testimony.

Their love for life did not deter them from
  death;
therefore, rejoice, you heavens
and you that dwell therein.

Revelation 11:17-18; 12:10b-12a

Prayer of Praise to God Our Father

Mighty and awesome are Your works,
Lord God Almighty.
Righteous and true are Your ways,
O King of the nations.
Who would dare refuse to honor You
or to offer You the glory due to Your Name,
  O Lord?
Since You alone are holy,
all nations shall come and worship in Your
  presence.
Your wonderful deeds are clearly evident.

Revelation 15:3-4

Prayer of Joy on the Lamb's
Wedding Day

Alleluia!
Salvation, glory, and power belong to our
  God,
for His judgments are marked by truth and
  justice.
Praise our God, all you His servants,
the small and the great who worship Him.

Alleluia!
The Lord is King,
our God, the Almighty.
Let us rejoice and be glad,
and give Him glory.
For this is the wedding day of the Lamb;
His bride has adorned herself for the nuptials.
She has been given a gown to wear,
brilliant white and made of the finest linen.

Revelation 19:1, 5-7

ANGELIC SALUTATION

(Hail Mary)

This prayer is added here as being substantially from the Bible (Luke 1:28; 2:42), although it was put together by the Church, which added the word Jesus (at the end of the first part) and the entire second part.

Hail, Mary,
full of grace,
the Lord is with you.
Blessed are you among women,
and blessed is the fruit of your womb, Jesus.

Holy Mary,
Mother of God,
pray for us sinners,
now and at the hour of our death.

INDEX OF PRAYER THEMES

(Bold type indicates the four major divisions of the book)